West of Wherevermore

AND OTHER ESSAYS

Donald Sidney-Fryer has written or edited the following books:

Poems in Prose, by Clark Ashton Smith (1965)
Etchings in Ivory, poems in prose by Robert E. Howard (1968)
Other Dimensions, short stories by Clark Ashton Smith (1970)
Songs and Sonnets Atlantean: The First Series (1971)
Selected Poems, omnibus by Clark Ashton Smith (1971)
The Last of the Great Romantic Poets, i.e., Clark Ashton Smith (1973)
Emperor of Dreams: A Clark Ashton Smith Bibliography (1978)
The Black Book of Clark Ashton Smith, his commonplace book (1979)
A Vision of Doom, poems by Ambrose Bierce (1980)
The City of the Singing Flame, tales by Clark Ashton Smith (1981)
The Last Incantation, tales by Clark Ashton Smith (1982)
The Monster of the Prophecy, tales by Clark Ashton Smith (1983)
Strange Shadows: The Uncollected Fiction and Essays of Clark Ashton Smith, edited by Steve Behrends with Donald Sidney-Fryer and Rah Hoffman (1989)
The Hashish-Eater; or, The Apocalypse of Evil, 1922 version, by Clark Ashton Smith (1990; with CD 2008 performed by D. Sidney-Fryer)
As Green as Emeraude: The Collected Poems of Margo Skinner (1990)
The Devil's Notebook (complete epigrams and apothegms) by Clark Ashton Smith, edited with Don Herron (1990)
Songs and Sonnets Atlantean: The Second Series (2003)
Gaspard de la Nuit, by Aloysius Bertrand, translation (2004)
Songs and Sonnets Atlantean: The Third Series (2005)
The Atlantis Fragments: The trilogy of "Songs and Sonnets Atlantean," omnibus (2008, 2009)
The Outer Gate: The Collected Poems of Nora May French (2009)
The Golden State Phastasticks: The California Romantics and Related Subjects: Collected Essays and Reviews, edited with Leo Grin and Alan Gullette (2011)
The Atlantis Fragments, The Novel: The Existing Chronicle: A Vision of the Final Days (2011)
Hobgoblin Apollo: The Autobiography of Donald Sidney-Fryer (2016)
Odds & Ends (poetry, 2016)
The Averoigne Chronicles, by Clark Ashton Smith, edited by Ron Hilger with Donald Sidney-Fryer (2016)
West of Wherevermore and Other Travel Writings (2016)
Aesthetics Ho! Essays on art, literature, and theatre (2017)
Ends and Odds (poetry, 2017)
The Case of the Light Fantastic Toe: The Romantic Ballet and Signor Maestro Cesare Pugni—A Chronicle and Source Book (2018)

WEST OF WHEREVERMORE

AND OTHER ESSAYS

———

Donald Sidney-Fryer

Hippocampus Press
———
New York

West of Wherevermore copyright © 2019 by Hippocampus Press.

Works by Donald Sidney-Fryer copyright © 2016, 2019 Donald Sidney-Fryer.

Grateful acknowledgment is made to Wade German for permission to reprint his poems "Château Névréant," "The Night Forrest," "Shadow and Silence," and "Hendecasyllabics" from *Dreams from a Black Nebula,* copyright © 2014 by Wade German for Hippocampus Press. Ditto to Donald Sidney-Fryer for his reviews "To the Stars and Beyond" (*Spectral Realms* No. 1, Summer 2014), "Enlightenment from the Outer Dark" (*Spectral Realms* No. 4, Winter 2016), and "A Journey Beyond All Journeys" (*Dead Reckonings* No. 22, Fall 2017); and his introduction, "Surrealism Is as Surrealism Does" from *The Lighthouse Above the Graveyard* by John Allen and Alan Gullette (Albany/Oakland: Dark Green Sun Press, 2016). Ditto to Alan Gullette for his poems "Poiema," "Giving Thanks," and "The Master Appeared" from *Reviving a Dead Priest* © 2018 by Alan Gullette for translucent books.

All rights reserved. Except for review purposes, no part of this book may be reproduced or transmitted in any form or by any means, electronic or mechanical, including photocopying, recording or by any information storage and retrieval system, without permission in writing from the publisher.

Published by Hippocampus Press
P.O. Box 641, New York, NY 10156
www.hippocampuspress.com

Cover artwork and design by Daniel V. Sauer, dansauerdesign.com. Hippocampus Press logo designed by Anastasia Damianakos.

First Edition
1 3 5 7 9 8 6 4 2

ISBN 978-1-61498-275-3

Contents

Introduction: "West of Wherevemore" 11
A Trip to Southeast Asia 13
A Sentimental Pilgrimage to Mother Egypt 51
An Interlude in Central America: El Salvador 97
A Trip to Hawaii and Micronesia 107
Time-Line Night at Beyond Baroque 123
Surrealism Is as Surrealism Does 129
To the Stars and Beyond 135
A Journey Beyond All Journeys 149
Enlightenment from the Outer Dark 163
An Account of Donaldo's Attendance at StokerCon in
    Providence, R.I. 171
In the Footsteps of the Masters 177
Musings Philosophical and Religious 181
The Miscellaneon 187

West of Wherevermore

*This collection of essays
on travel and other subjects
is dedicated to*

JOSEPH JACOBO CENDEJAS

Introduction: "West of Wherevemore"

"Follow the sunset, follow the sun, / Follow wherever the sun's rays run!" might make the motto for any pursuit or quest, search and research. Whether an expedition into unknown geography on planet Earth or an armchair safari into unknown realms of dream—let us call them dreamscapes—it involves the same principle, all petty or grandiose politics aside, but not poetics. We all seek poetry in various forms, whether traditional or non-traditional, whether outside of us as in everyday verifiable geography, or inside of us, reflecting our everyday lives and incarnations, whether recalled immediately or re-imagined. Imagined remains the operative word here. We cannot function without imagination in the midst of everyday life. But in particular we cannot function without imagination ostensibly in a story or history reflecting actual existence, or a purported history or experience in the lands of Otherwhere often reduplicating our everyday life. It is axiomatic that we first describe the unknown in terms of the known.

We do not discuss per se what might be called the dark side of things and ourselves, that is, in and of themselves. The dark side forms part of the inevitable whole, but is not more potent than the light or positive side, which is where many people strive to exist, to stay balanced and sane in the most fundamental manner possible. But whereas everyday geography, everyday circumstances, demand that we pay sedulous attention to things in a practical manner, imagination makes different as well as distinctive demands on us if we would accost the geography of Otherwhere. Thus it is with these considerations in mind that we invite the reader to contemplate the issues raised in the essays that follow, no less the poetry that follows the essays, but conceived in the same spirit of possibility or impossibility.

Many great thinkers have stressed the strategic importance of dreams and dreaming in our lives, Albert Einstein most notably in modern times, that is, of the last few hundred years, the late nineteenth century on into the first few decades of the twenty-first century. Before we can realize things in a practical fashion, we must make them real in our minds, in our dreaming or thinking about them in reverie.

D. SIDNEY-FRYER

Wherevermore, East Sandwich,
Cape Cod, Massachusetts,
Friday morning, 23 March 2018.

A Trip to Southeast Asia

Special Note

This report on a recent voyage (from Southern California to Southeast Asia and back) is dedicated—with love, piety, gratitude, and remembrance—to the late great Robin Rowe Reynolds II, of Sacramento, California, cherished friend and generous patron over many years, whose bequest to the writer made that exotic safari possible.

TO WHOM IT MAY CONCERN

May this report seem cogent! I recalled most of it from memory, and from a few notes that I took while I was in Southeast Asia. I wrote it during 3-24 May, a period of dental and surgical traumas. Then during 19-20-21 May, Rah had guests, one from Paris. Recovering from surgery, I could not really take part in the socializing. Moreover, I would not have had company at that particular time, but had no choice.

On 3 May a marginal tooth declared its abscess. Under the aegis of UCLA's dental clinic, antibiotics reduced the infection and the pain. The tooth came out on 19 May, with little bleeding, and the gum healed almost at once. The bone will take about six months. Meanwhile at Kaiser in West L.A. surgery took place.

A polyp in my colon, nestled in an awkward fold, could not yield to the usual procedure by Dr. Yuh. He gave the task to Dr. Farooqui, a superb surgeon, who had removed the large tumor then in my colon on 9 June 2008. He now removed the reluctant polyp, and successfully. Even if classified as minor surgery, it still takes it out of the patient.

The sequence: pre-op, Tuesday, 11 May; the op, Thursday, 13 May; the post-op, Monday, 24 May. Some limited bleeding lingered on for about a week, and has now stopped. I have been able to walk my usual fast pace the last few days, at last. Although I cannot stay in the water, I can swim or dive for a brief time. The water is finally comfortable (anent temperature), hooray!

Writing this report helped me take my mind off dental and post-surgical discomfort (Vicodin also helped, and quite a bit), but concentration and continuity became a problem due to all the interruptions (argh). I had to do a lot of rereading of what I had already written before I could commence writing again.

Donaldo, 29 May 2010.

Apart from the pain in the ass, I never know just when I shall need to go the bathroom, so I can't stray too far from home these days. Lately that dilemma has improved. I'll be singularly relieved to return to my usual bathroom routine, ahem!

A REPORT ON A TRIP TO SOUTHEAST ASIA,
28 February–16 April 2010.

(Thailand & Cambodia.)

CHRONOLOGY: Although I may mention dates and such like during my report, I have given here at the start, for easy reference, the trip's overall chronology.

28 February: Flight to Bangkok, China Air Lines.
2-4 March: Bangkok, Swan Hotel.
5-7 March: Ayutthaya, Ayothaya Hotel.
8-9 March: Bangkok, Swan Hotel.
10-24 March, Cambodia: Phnom Penh, Siem Reap, Angkor.
    10-13 March: Phnom Penh, Hotel Cara.
    14-22 March: Siem Reap, Monoreach Angkor Hotel.
    23-March: Phnom Penh, Hotel Cara.
24-25 March: Bangkok, Swan Hotel.
26 March-13 April: Koh Samui, Baan Shadis Samui.
13 April: Bangkok, Swan Hotel.
14 April: Return to Los Angeles via China Air Lines.

    I, the author, prepare this little report for a small circle of friends who have expressed an interest in reading such an account. Even if I have returned home now to Westchester (L.A. just north of LAX, L.A.'s largest and most utilized airport) for almost three full weeks, this is my first chance to sit down and redact the account on paper. Otherwise, no writing apart from a dozen personal letters mailed in response to the letters from friends found here at my return. While I have already done quite a lot, many chores exist whenever I return from a trip, especially a long one like that to Southeast Asia, lasting almost seven weeks, not quite two months: for example, touching up the house, checking on the property outside (watering, pruning, etc.), walking to and shopping at our little local supermarket, post office, and the nearest major intersection, Sepulveda and Manchester, and always, or often, taking care of dear old Rah, now but half a year away from turning NINETY. I am more or less happy to find myself at home, but already I am homesick for Southeast Asia and the wonderful people who live there. How different is the tone or feel of Buddhist society, especially as compared with the major countries reflecting Christianity and Islam, the two greatest monotheistic religions! Such countries, no doubt about it, represent the most violent, aggressive, and self-righteous people on the planet, who feel that they have the moral right to kill people who do not share their dogmas or other values! No religion has ever stopped people from doing the most ghastly things to each other, but the two Buddhist countries that I visited (that is, their peoples) have a sweetness, a gentility, a mutual deference, and an harmoniousness that I have not found anywhere else. A humanistic paradise!

I experienced this revelation not so much at once, of course, but gradually, day by day, not just (and obviously) because I traveled in a privileged way as a foreigner, a tourist, a guest, in those countries but above all from observing, and living among, the same peoples. The routine flight itself went very well, Déesse merci!—the flight attendants kept us well fed and responded to questions or requests however they could, and the passenger passed the time watching movies on those tiny TV screens, reading books or magazines, or just plain sleeping. Happily I can sleep in coach, plane or train, or at least lose partial consciousness, almost the same—although one always yearns to lie prone on the floor or in a bed! After landing for the final time, and at Bangkok, on the flight from L.A.—after stopping first at Taipei, Taiwan, and second at Hong Kong, China, that is, after some twenty hours of total flight time, and then for several additional hours during the layovers in Taipei and Hong Kong—nothing dominated my consciousness except how tired I felt. Once I had passed through immigration and customs, and changed my American dollars for Siamese baht (32 to the dollar), I sought a counter nearby where I arranged to stay at the Swan Hotel for several nights, an excellent hostelry with midrange prices. I needed to get to bed fast. I felt very tired. I also arranged for 500 baht to take a taxi, or taximeter, from the immense airport terminal to the Swan Hotel, a mile or so southeast of the old Grand Palace, and east of the Chao Phraya river.

The reader needs to know right here at the start something that nobody or no guidebook makes clear about the pronunciation of certain letter combinations in English translation, *ph* and *th:* simply pronounce them as *p* or *t.* The *ph* is not an *f,* the *th* is neither of the two *th* sounds in English. We had not driven far through open country when we came upon Bangkok's outskirts. It must have taken the taximeter about an hour of driving (making two toll stops) at 60 miles an hour (the legal limit) to reach the hotel sometime early or midafternoon. The Thai capital covers an enormous territory, and although most of the buildings average two to four or five levels, great monolithic skyscrapers increasingly dominate the skyline the closer one gets to Central Bangkok. At a rough guess Bangkok must cover the same amount of terrain as London or New York City. The overall urban ensemble impressed and amazed me. Wow, Bangkok is BIG!

For all its apparent exoticism (as noted by outsiders), the capital and the country are modern, whereas Phnom Penh and Cambodia have just recently recovered from the long and horrible years of civil war, 1970-98 (essentially ending with Pol Pot's death in 1998 in Anlong Veng near the central Cambodian border on the north), and especially from the brutal governance of the Khmer Rouge, 1975-78/79. As soon as we arrived at the hotel and I registered, I mounted to my room with my two bags (a medium-sized overnight bag that can fit into the overhead bin of any passenger plane, and a shoulder bag with essentials that I always keep with me). Once in the sanctuary-oasis of my chamber, I undressed, took a shower, went to bed (what a relief!), and fell asleep at once. When I awoke, I did some calisthenics, donned my trunks, and took the first of many swims in the hotel's deep, large, and ever so refreshing pool.

The hotel has a nice little restaurant, with a cook on duty not only for the breakfast buffet but for lunch and supper as well. I ate there that first night, probably fish and chips and salad. As I would find out the next morning at my first breakfast, almost all hotels except for the very fanciest ones handle breakfast as a buffet, ideal for feeding large groups of people fast and efficiently. Thanks to the air-conditioning, I felt quite comfortable in my room, but as it soon began to seem cold to me, I learned to keep it at minimal cool. The hotels have a neat system for not wasting energy when a chamber has no guest. As the guest enters the room, he inserts a plastic handle (attached to the key) into a special slot about level with his head. This activates the air-conditioning. When the guest leaves the room to go into the hotel at large, or outside the building, he removes the key from the special slot, and the air-conditioning turns off in a minute or so. The chamber keeps cool for a while, especially if the guest returns fairly soon, say, within 20 or 30 minutes.

Coming from L.A., where the winter temperatures (comparatively mild vis-à-vis the rest of the U.S.) had long since yielded to the 60s or 70s during the day and to 50 at night (Fahrenheit), the tropical climate seemed much hotter than anticipated. Bangkok lies about 1000 miles north of the equator. The overtly cool season runs from December through February, even if (apparently) the monsoon months (usually October–November) average cooler than the hottest months of April–May, or the only a little less hot months of June–September. From the end of February through March on into mid-April, when the greatest heat peaks and maintains itself through May, the weather gradually warms up.

Quite unexpectedly this year, the great heat returned at once, taking everyone by surprise, including the natives and the resident expatriates. Flying west from L.A. to Bangkok, the airplane passenger loses a day. Flying east back to L.A., the flyer gains a day. Flying some 10,000 miles from L.A. to Taipei and then another 2,000 miles to Bangkok, I was taken by complete surprise by how that much warmer the tropics actually impact the traveler physically with their much greater heat and moisture, their normal condition. Even if I usually love the heat, suddenly 30 or 40 degrees all at once hit me harder than anticipated. HOT! Living in Sacramento from 1975 to 1998—a town to which I moved from San Francisco, so I could have the advantages of warmth or great heat about half the year (say, May through October or November), and getting beautifully adjusted to that warmth or heat—I was no stranger to heat per se but not at such a fast rate!

The breakfast buffet is open 6 or 6:30 to 9:00 A.M. (the time varies from hotel to hotel but not by much), and offers both Thai and Western-style food, the Thai rarely spicy, the natives understanding quite well that most Westerners don't like or can't endure spicy food. The local food in general is tasty and inviting, with many vegetables, noodles, rice (a staple food throughout the East), and fresh fruit (usually pineapple, watermelon, and other melons). Western-style deli ham, bacon, fried eggs, and toast are also available, plus coffee and tea. Most hotels repeat this basic menu wherever the tourist goes. Since it comes with the room, I ate the same breakfast day after day (a little monotonous but otherwise okay), the menu satisfied me. I'm not a food connoisseur.

I would eat a big meal again only in the evening (at the hotel or somewhere else), accompanied by the usual beers available, Heineken, Singha, and Chang, the two latter being local beers, good light lagers. Although available, wines whether by bottle or by glass proved too costly for this ever frugal or financially limited traveler. On one occasion the food manager treated me to a glass, the remaining residue of a previously opened bottle. It was good. Sometimes I would eat a small lunch, or in my room a small snack of some type. The management in most hotels thoughtfully provides in or near each room's little fridge such items as beer, fruit juice, mineral or ice water, Coca Cola, Sprite or Fresca, plus potato chips and candy bars. A little menu with prices sits on or near the fridge, and anything consumed is noted and added to the bill that the guest usually pays on checking out of the hotel. The guest is perfectly free to bring onto the premises a bottle of spirits with which to make cocktails, etc.

I had landed at Bangkok on 2 March, and after breakfast on the 3rd I took a little tour of the capital with a professional tourist guide Jira (licensed, she had obtained an university degree to work in the Thai tourism business, which provides about 25% of the country's GDP). A charming and amiable woman, she indicated the wide range of tourist options available near Bangkok, none of which interested me because I had already worked out my probable itinerary. The tour was free, but followed by visits to a jewelry store, a haberdashery, and a travel business, as all part of the free tour, an accustomed prearrangement, none of which enticed me, the frugal traveler. I still had to pay the guide, a charge that I figured as 500 baht, which price Jira confirmed when I asked her at the end of the tour for her personal charge. The commercial part of the tour need not detain us; the main or cultural part claims prime time.

Mobile, Jira supplied the driver and auto, paying him out of her own fee, not ungenerous as payment to her, in exchange for only a few hours' work. We began about 9:00 A.M. and finished about 1:00

P.M., my first real experience of the celebrated heat of the tropics. We spent most of our time at the old Grand Palace, whose walled compound boasts many magnificent palaces, temples, and other structures. The Royal Family of Thailand resides elsewhere, in another large but more modern compound, and uses the older palace enclosure (some 500 by 700 meters) mostly for ceremonial purposes. Much of the architecture presents the fantastic and brilliant appearance familiar from photos and movies. The temple area, the area mostly open to the public, attracts the greatest part of both tourists and Buddhist pilgrims. The public has permission to visit some of the palaces adapted as museums. The most spectacular site remains the fantasticated Wat Phrat Kaew, the Temple of the diminutive Emerald Buddha (probably made of jasper or jade, not of emerald), guarded by the very large and characteristic statues of mythical giants daemonic and rather frightening in appearance. They stand with immense maces or swords before them resting on the ground.

Like everyone else, Jira and I took off our shoes before we entered the interior coruscating with gold, gems, and tiny mirrors. While doing the same herself, she told me how to get down on my knees, bowing deeply with hands clasped together (fingers upward) in prayer, the standard gesture of respect whether to gods or humans in Buddhist lands and in India. I had now become quite heated, and I lacked patience and energy for the commercial part of the tour. We finished with that as fast as I could go through the ordeal, rather to the chagrin of my guide and the business people, her allies! I bought nothing and expressed my lack of interest in the strongest terms. I paid her off, and the driver took me back to the hotel. I took his card, however, and told him that if I needed a private driver I would use him. I had not traveled some 12,000 miles to encounter or tolerate the same kind of business behavior in my native country. Bah!

As an aside I should mention something maybe perfectly obvious about travel and tourism, and in pointed reference to my trip to Southeast Asia. I had planned the trip not just to visit Angkor, the old capital and center of the Khmer Empire that flourished from 802 to 1431 C.E., but also to visit some of Thailand's most notable sites and monuments, generally located in and around Bangkok. It was a hard choice between Egypt (fascinating to me since almost as early as I could read) and Angkor in Cambodia (which came into my consciousness much later). I chose Angkor over Egypt because of the much greater closeness in time, culturally and linguistically, between the Khmers of today and those who created Angkor and its empire, only something less than 600 years. Starting with the Arab conquest of the seventh century C.E., the Egyptians no longer speak their own language (still preserved but only in the liturgy of the Coptic Church), and something like 2000 years divides them from 323–30 C.E., their last period of greatness and independence under the Ptolemies.

Thus, compared to the Egyptians, a much greater closeness unites the present Khmers and those of their imperial past, and this in and of itself presents a fascinating attraction, making me choose Cambodia. However, concerning the obvious point mentioned above, in order to visit the Angkorian monuments, much displacement has to take place first, "displacement" of time, money, and energy, not to mention endless pre-arrangements and other plans, as well as negotiations with other people in person and over the telephone. This is true of any kind of extensive travel, but especially so when it involves a remote destination halfway around the world! Look how long it has taken me to make this obvious point in what I term at the start as just "this little report"!

On a note of profound gratitude, I should mention here what made my sojourn in Southeast Asia possible. For many years I worked for a wonderful family in Sacramento—son, father, and mother—who became unique and generous friends to me, eternal blessings upon them all. The mother died some time ago, the son still is very much alive and prospering, and the father died in July of 2009. Through his son he very kindly left me a bequest of several thousand dollars, and this alone made my whole marvelous experience unto and within Southeast Asia a reality. Whether visiting the Grand Palace in Bangkok or some other locale, the members of this family often accompanied me in my interior mental or psychic space. In other words, I often thought of them during my trip!

I should also mention another feature of interest for Anglophones, a real advantage for Brits and Americans thanks to the existence first of the British Empire and now the British Commonwealth and then of the commercial and military dominance of the U.S. (since World

War II). It seems as it almost everyone speaks English, including nonnative English speakers of Europe, the Middle East, and the Far East, not to mention Africa. In fact, they often speak it better than many Americans, grammatically and otherwise. Outside Southeast Asia the outsider can't take those languages anywhere else except to expatriate communities in the U.S. and elsewhere. Nevertheless, it certainly helps to speak a few phrases of their respective languages whether in Myanmar/Burma, Thailand/Siam, Cambodia, Laos, and Vietnam. The traveler can still hear some French in Laos, Vietnam, and Cambodia, but much less in the last-named.

On 4 March I took what would emerge as the first of many little exploratory strolls in the general vicinage of my hotel, noting (inter alia) not far away the French Embassy: a handsome, good-sized mosque; and especially the celebrated Oriental Hotel associated with writers such as Joseph Conrad, Somerset Maugham, Noel Coward, Graham Greene, James Michener, and Gore Vidal. Because Bangkok became established and then developed in an unplanned way, not laid out on a grid, the city very much rewards little explorations on foot, especially divagations, with surprising and enjoyable discoveries. A particular source of delight: often embowered with trees, bushes, and gardens (kitchen and otherwise), the old-style wooden houses from the 1800s (once everywhere, and characteristic of old Bangkok), usually one story tall with sloping roofs and huge wide shutters opening out upward awning-style, the structures usually raised up high by one story's height (for protection from the downpour and splatter of the monsoon rains). The residents often utilize the ground level underneath these old houses (whether paved or not) for storage or for hanging out in the cool shade at various times of the day or evening. The sun comes up around 6:00 A.M. and goes down around 6:00 P.M., with no real twilight. Before air-conditioning people usually sat or lay quiet during the height of the day's heat from noon to late afternoon, as in most tropical countries.

Trains and buses do not always run on schedule, and the train that I hoped to take to Ayutthaya at 9:30 A.M. did not leave until 11:30 from the central railroad station, reaching the old capital about 1:00 P.M. I passed through some lovely verdant countryside, dotted with temples, towns, and estates. Often splendid and striking with white and gold in addition to their fantasticated roofs, Buddhist temples usually stand behind ceremonial walls and have a general resemblance to one another inside their equally glittering compounds. With their colonnades, grand portals, and multiple roofs decorated fantastically, the temples make a brave and welcome show; they are as ubiquitous as Christian churches in Europe. We finally but finally reached Ayutthaya. Too tired and hot to look around for cheap digs, I took a taxi to the nearest hostelry.

This turned out to be the fanciest place in town, the Ayothaya Hotel, on a main street in the eastern part of the far-spreading city. Of course, a later town has grown up around the tall multiple spires of the old capital with its impressive ruins. The main hotel cost rather too much for me, and so the manager Samphong gave me a standard room in the annex at the back beyond a parking lot. Once ensconced in my chamber, I ate some food that I had with me, but had a shower first of all. I then took a much-needed nap, huddling under my blanket in the cold, air-conditioned room. When I woke, I did my usual exercises, got dressed, and went downstairs in the early evening to have dinner. The usual pattern for me at all the hotels where I would stay turned out the same: only two meals a day, a big breakfast buffet early morning and a regular dinner at night. The Ayothaya has a fancy dining room just within from the elegant lobby. Although the hotel has an indoor pool and gym, I never used them and contented myself with a regular (cool) shower every now and then, particularly when I would come in after my usual half-day outside from midmorning to early afternoon, a half-day only due to the great heat. On Saturday morning, 6 March, after breakfast, the manager Samphong recommended a local tuk-tuk driver to me for ease of transport around the vast site of old Ayutthaya. Only in this case the tuk-tuk comprised more a kind of small pick-up, a small roofed truck open on all sides with two long benches facing each other the length of the vehicle, mountable at the rear by small steps.

The driver Noy (Noy Waraporn, or Thai style, Waraporn Noy) emerged as a warm and jolly woman who would carry me around the ruins and other monuments for that Saturday and Sunday, and also take me to a bus station on Monday, to return to Bangkok. If you should go to Ayutthaya, do use her services, Tuk-Tuk Tour Ayutthaya No. 549, telephone 084-77667572—she provides great service! Her professional companionship and advice would make my sojourn in the old capital a real joy. We would meet mid-morning and would then tour on into the early afternoon, the same procedure that I would follow while in Cambodia at Siem Reap and Angkor. Although I did get used to the heat somewhat, I stayed in the shade as much as possible and would return to my air-conditioned chamber in the hotel, taking a cool shower, with a genuine sense of relief!

Simply driving with the Lady Noy, the perimeter access road here and there (we covered the entire length of it on Sunday) revealed the enormous territory once encompassed by the walls of what—from descriptions written in the 1600s and 1700s by early European traders—sounds like a Venice of the Far East, rich and resplendent, environed by rivers and crossed by canals. The town with all its real, its fabled wealth proved an irresistible prize to the Burmese, who had sacked the place once before. Under a strong warrior king, they besieged Ayutthaya for a year and then destroyed it in 1767. Looting it completely, they devastated the town and wiped out the people, forcing the survivors further south, eventually to a locale that became Bangkok. The Thai naturally have never forgotten this terrible event, and while they may welcome the Burmese individually, many Thai still regard them collectively with horror.

The kingdom of and around Ayutthaya maintained its existence from the mid-1300s to the mid-1700s, that is for 416 years. Although I thrilled to what a glittering capital this must have become ere its fall, the devastation wrought by the Burmese, including the murder of its inhabitants after surviving their siege for a year, made and makes my blood run cold. Noy took me to various temples whose compounds preserved many Buddhas large and small, and the high spires of many stupas. The traveler can still walk up into those that have interiors and are not solid, as many remain. My favorite site lay somewhere in the northeastern section, an immense temple area filled with the remains of red-brick buildings yet intact, probably once covered with white-painted plaster. I lingered here the longest, attempting to picture what appearance it must have presented in all its glory. Farther to the west Noy took me next to the largest compound of all with many edifices, centered around a modern temple splendid with white and gold. Without going inside, I walked completely around the structure, peering inside its four great portals, each at the cardinal points of the compass, the main one on the east.

From this modern enclave we drove to a certain special milieu somewhere in the south-central area, a locale where people can take rides on the backs of elephants (very well treated, incidentally), one short ride and one long ride. I took the short ride and decided that, apart from the sheer exoticism of it, walking turns out to be faster and easier. However, if one had no choice but an elephant ride, it would make an efficient mode of travel over long distances, as through the jungle. Nonetheless, I loved being around the elephants, and the bulls are BIG. People mounted or dismounted the elephant backs from high thatched platforms. It made a fantastic sight to see the elephants with mahouts and passengers going north and then back in an endless procession. The last place for that day that the Lady Noy took me lay way to the west, not far from the Chao Phraya river, a very large Buddha lying on his side. For a small price to the Buddha keepers, and under Noy's guidance, I offered several lotus blossoms and incense sticks before the image and applied several pieces of gold leaf to the statue, all this to invite good fortune. I made the suitable bows and hand gestures, and the whole sweet ceremony gave me a good and pleasant feeling.

Sunday went much more quietly. I had not taken enough cash out of a local bank (I had not yet graduated to ATM's!) earlier on Saturday, and the money went faster than anticipated, to give Noy a sizeable tip in addition to what she charged me for the day or half-day. At first she took me to places requiring a small outlay of cash, and when she finally grasped my limited means, she then took me to ruins requiring no admission, or whose external extent I could negotiate with no thought of money. As our final excursion we drove the entire length of the perimeter access road that runs around the vast overall site of the ancient capital. What an enormous terrain that old Ayutthaya once occupied! By this time the dirtiness and vehicular pollution was making me near ill, and so we made it an early day. If the latter poses a real problem in areas of Thailand, it becomes even worse in Cambodia, especially pollution from trash: those awful plastic bags that we have exported around the world!

I had mulled over the possibilities of reaching Cambodia via Siam by bus and/or train, going into the land of the Khmers via Anlong Veng, but after the late train going to Ayutthaya, I decided against it. Too much of a chance of being delayed in too many places, plus endless negotiation with Noy to have her pick me up in the late morning and take me to a bus station, so I could bus back to Bangkok. I did not want to run the risk again of arriving someplace late, as I did on Friday. On Monday morning all went smoothly. Noy helped me to buy my ticket, I gave her a handsome tip, I kissed her hand, and she gave me a great big hug. Gosh, it made me feel so good! Then we parted, and after the long but rapid bus ride back to Bangkok, and then an inexpensive taximeter ride, I found myself back at the Swan Hotel (it had begun to feel like home) for several nights, luxuriating in its wonderful swimming pool once again! What a relief it provided against the great heat that lay heavy everywhere.

LE CAMBODGE ET ANGKOR

A little French seems rather apt here. Gamboge, or gambodge, an earlier French form of the name, has established itself in English as a somewhat rare word, reflecting one of the two former or continuing exports from that country, forest products and rice. In this case, to quote from *Webster's New Collegiate Dictionary* of 1951, it denotes a color reddish-yellow in hue, of high saturation and high brilliance, deriving from an orange-red gum (a tree resin) used by artists as a yellow or yellow-orange pigment. To some extent this word reflects not only early French trade and other connections with Cambodia, but also the French protectorate that the French set up over the country during 1864–1953. Without that protectorate Cambodia might have disappeared off the map. In 1794 Siam took control of one-third or one-fourth of Cambodia's territory, chiefly the northwestern provinces of Battambang, Preah Vihear, and Siem Reap, and thus Angkor itself, the old enlarged heart of the Khmer Empire. In 1907 France negotiated the return of the three provinces to Cambodia. Interestingly enough, Siam and Vietnam have strategically assisted Cambodia at other times or provided refuge for the Khmers fleeing some inimical régime.

Rather than reaching Angkor by an indirect route, via Siam and Anlong Veng, near the northern Khmer border, I had decided while in Ayutthaya to go there by the usual and easiest mode already and conveniently put into operation: fly via Bangkok Airways from Siam's capital to Phnom Penh; spend a few days in the Cambodian capital; take the air-conditioned bus (about six hours) to Siem Reap, and get settled there in some hotel; go out every day or so to Angkor via tuk-tuk driver (the local taxi service at so much per little tour or big tour). The flight to Phnom Penh takes only about an hour or so; to return to Bangkok, I would need only to reverse the process. I decided to spend two weeks total in Cambodia, 10–24 March. The Swan Hotel's manager negotiated my airplane ticket for me and it required a whole half-hour, many blessings upon Supisith.

As preparation for my trip I did much advance reading during September 2009 into February 2010, many books on the history and culture of Siam and Cambodia, borrowing them from UCLA's unparalleled Research Library. I also obtained my own copies of the Lonely Planet Guidebooks to those countries for my own use; for my money, they are the best guides to any country. I also purchased their *Southeast Asia Phrasebook* (the five countries). During that brief stay of 9–10 March at the Swan, Supisith, not knowing that I spoke French and am half-French in ancestry, introduced me to a handsome and amiable gentleman, Michel Drouet, who works as some kind of attaché for the French Embassy in Bangkok, traveling on some kind of official and/or commercial business among the various French embassies and consulates in Southeast Asia as well as Malaysia, Indonesia, and Australia. Speaking French, discussing French art and culture, etc. (a great pleasure for me), we passed several quite agreeable visits together in the hotel, and also in an excellent restaurant not far away to the west (specializing in the best fish entrées), the Café Harmonique, on one of Bangkok's many little streets or paved alleys. He had invited me to stay with his family while in Phnom Penh; this did not work out, but Michel very kindly arranged for me to stay at an excellent midrange hotel there, the Hotel Cara.

Lacking easy access to a phone, I had enlisted Supisith's help in setting up my ticket to Cambodia and back. With his cell phone and his laptop computer, he was able to do this in a way impossible to me.

His full name is Supisith Visaruthamrongkul. Even with all his experience it still took half an hour to negotiate that ticket. Had I done it myself, I would have ended up a nervous wreck. All such negotiations make me inexplicably nervous, almost panic-struck. I am not afraid or ashamed to admit it. My neighbor friend Marie Hedlund with her computer had generously set up my trip to Bangkok and back, sparing me that horror as well.

Even though quite eager to arrive at Siem Reap and Angkor, I wanted to spend some few days in Phnom Penh. Overall the time that I passed there emerged as worthwhile and even fascinating, Wednesday through Saturday, 10-13 March. I found this town west of the Mekong river dirty and full of trash, with terrible air quality (all those tuk-tuks and motorbikes, plus trucks and cars). Easy of access, the main riverfront thoroughfare, Sisowath Quai, takes the tourist to the National Museum and Art Institute, just north of the Khmer Royal Palace. The palace compound is open to the public only within its temple precinct at the southeast corner, the latter including the celebrated Silver Pagoda. Measuring 400 by 400 metres, the walled-in palace area compares favorably (albeit smaller by about one half) with Bangkok's Grand Palace, measuring 500 by 700 metres. It presents a fantastic appearance no less impressive than its Thai counterpart.

During my four days in the Khmer capital, I did a lot of walking from mid-morning to early afternoon along the riverfront, starting at my hotel only a little inland and proceeding every day as far south as the Royal Palace, then returning via an inland route that went by the small hill (the original Phnom Penh) dominated by the striking, high-spiring temple of Wat Phnom, surrounded by a lovely park full of graceful trees. To avoid vendors and hustlers, I promenaded along the riverfront park, putting me in the hot sun, but I do not regret the greater privacy that resulted. The then shady side of Sisowath Quai, on the west, embodied a solid wall of architecture apart from the embouchures of the streets coming into the corniche. I would stop on occasion, but usually at the walk's end, for a beer or a rum and coke at a bar, a restaurant, or a combination of the two. Of course, the real cool-off would come when I returned to my hotel and took a shower. Oh blessèd, refreshing downpour of water!

After returning from my walk around noon on Saturday, 13

March, at my request Mme. Kim, who runs the front desk in the lobby (and possibly the entire hotel on a de facto basis), arranged not only my round-trip ticket on the air-conditioned bus that leaves around mid-morning, but also my stay, 14–22 March, at the Monoreach Angkor Hotel, which stands on the north side of the road from the main part of Siem Reap to the airport that lies to the northwest. At that hotel I would live in a small "suite" consisting of an elegant chamber with full bathroom and entrance hall, at less than half the price for what the room commands during the main tourist season, December through February.

This represented a great savings for me, the only provision being that I had to spend the full nine nights at that hotel only. This turned out a bit awkward, because the hotel stands about a mile or more (not at all convenient for walking) outside the older and more charming part of Siem Reap, where the traveler finds most of the bars and eateries especially active at night. Still, I could always hire a tuk-tuk to take me back and forth inexpensively, and I could not complain about the bargain. I must express here my gratitude to Mme. Kim at the Hotel Cara for her strategic help.

Thus I found myself ensconced in one of the fanciest hotels of my life by late Sunday afternoon, 14 March; and after a short nap I took the first of innumerable swims in the hotel's rather small but adequate swimming pool beautifully laid out on the hotel's eastern side. The bus from Phnom Penh had passed (to the east of the huge fresh-water lake, or inland sea, the Tonle Sap) through an almost completely flat country made up of small towns, villages, farms, and walled estates. Off and on during the long bus ride I would fall asleep while trying to read an unusual book given to me by a friend. Despite all the trash (those awful plastic bags), the green and fertile countryside provided quite a welcome relief after three days and four nights in a big crowded city, a big city nonetheless not without its attractions.

At last I found myself in place to visit the fabled Angkor, and from a secure and even luxurious base. The distance from Siem Reap, however, made it impractical in terms of time to walk there and back. Thus, on Monday, 15 March, when a young man on the breakfast-buffet staff, Pisay, or Vong Pisay, came up to me and asked how I would go back and forth to Angkor, I replied that I had made no arrangements, and certainly not with any pre-packaged bus tour. Then he asked me if I would consider using a local tuk-tuk driver whom he knew, a friend. I said yes. As I had already discovered, going from the aeroport to the hotel in Phnom Penh, the local or Cambodian tuk-tuk consists of a motorbike pulling a small two-wheel carriage or cab, but roofed and open on all sides; and the two seats face each other front to back. Pisay phoned his friend, Ong or Hong (actually Dit-Kimhong), and I would meet him around mid-morning near the front of the hotel. Pisay had kindly arranged it all.

Hong emerged as a slender, diffident, but appealing young man in his early thirties, and as I discovered on Tuesday, the 16th, he was married with two children—his wife stayed at home to care for them, a boy of six and a girl of nine. He had passed about a decade as a monk, a vocation that he left to resume life but not as a monk, as he later told me. He would provide now my transport back and forth to Angkor and elsewhere for the rest of my sojourn in Siem Reap during 15-22 March. I would now have a full week to spend in this general vicinity. I felt elated in spite of the challenge from the great heat.

A few random observations about the people whom I had met so far in Southeast Asia, people who appeared no less attractive than the land that nurtured them. If the Thai seem somewhat smaller than Americans and Europeans, then the Khmer seem tiny, and the young adults appear irresistibly cute. I say this advisedly because they do not attract me sexually. Their features are less sharp than those of Westerners, but less snub or broad than those of black Africans. In general the Thai and the Khmer are handsome and well-made, slight and slender. Combining their good looks with their extraordinary cheerfulness, they make very good company for a fact, whether old or young.

Covering overall an immense territory of 120 square miles, Angkor served as the heart, the center, of an even vaster empire extending over the whole of Southeast Asia, excluding Burma but including the northern third of the Thai-Malay peninsula. Interestingly enough, modern Siam covers almost exactly the same terrain, excluding not only modern Burma but also modern Cambodia, Laos, and Vietnam. The Khmer Empire dominated this area for more than six centuries, 802-1431, and only six centuries divide the modern Khmers and the modern tourist from that period of mostly undisputed greatness.

Just as ancient Egypt functioned as the mother of civilization for the eastern (if not the entire) Mediterranean, so did the Khmer Empire provide the model of a successful state for the then contemporary and later societies in Southeast Asia, Champa, Vietnam, Laos, Siam, and Burma, among others. Strongly but selectively influenced by Indic trade, life, culture, and religion, ancient Cambodia turned into its own highly original entity, as its monuments attest. During their six centuries of dominance the ancient Khmers built hundreds of temples and other major sites, not to mention thousands of shrines dispersed over an immense territory. Exploring and restoring just some of the major sites alone represents a tremendous and a colossal task. Archaeology remains a very expensive enterprise. Not only have many NGOs (non-governmental organizations) from other countries assisted Cambodia in recovering from the many years of civil war (including the ghastly regime of the Khmer Rouge), but many outside nations are aiding in the ongoing task, the supreme challenge, of restoring many major sites, nations such as France (first and foremost), Germany, China, Japan, the U.S., etc.

With such a wealth of sites to visit, even spread out over a week, I realized that I had to exercise a real selectivity to encompass either certain major sites or a variety of other locales in and around the ancient city locale of Angkor Thom. Sort of pre-planned, sort of improvised, anent the agenda, I let Hong and circumstances ultimately decide on some choices, as it provided more of a sense of adventure. I also decided in advance to spend no more than half a day per excursion via tuk-tuk into Angkor's enormous archaeological park, from mid-morning to early afternoon, given the great heat that had returned much faster than usual or expected.

Even if it may turn out a big disappointment, an anticlimax, to some of my readers, I shall not go into raptures of description or enmarvelment about the sites that I managed to visit. Any number of publishers have brought out any number of books about Angkor, some of them art books of great size, distinction, and authority—abundantly illustrated with stunning color photos—as put together by expert archaeological writers and first-rate creative photographers. People have laid waste their powers to do justice to places like Angkor: I have no intention to lay waste my limited powers that way. I am not competing with these worthies. Rather I urge the curious reader, seriously interested, to seek such books out at their nearest university or public library and study them there.

Thus, in reporting on my visits to Angkor, I shall content myself with brief general reports on the sites of choice intermixed with my personal impressions. But first I must state: what wonders has the École Française d'Extrême Orient (the French School of the Far East), EFEO, not achieved in clearing so many monuments from the encroaching or investing tropical jungle, and in patiently and painstakingly restoring and reconstructing them? It originally set up the foundation for all future archaeological work, and it did overall a top-notch job. It makes me proud to be part French, in fact a good one-half!

As it evolved, the deal that I worked out with Hong for his tuk-tuk services came out as follows: I would pay him for the equivalent of a little tour ($16.00), and not of a big tour ($20.00), per day. Since I was hiring him for only a half-day, we arranged in addition that he would pick me around 6:00 P.M., take me into the main part of Siem Reap, where I would select a restaurant for my evening meal (allowing an hour or so), after which he would pick me up again and return me to my hotel. Overall this arrangement emerged as gratifying to both driver and passenger. This is how my impromptu schedule turned out for 15–22 March.

A few more preliminary words. The tuk-tuk driver can travel via several routes to reach Angkor. The ride to and fro possesses quite a bit of charm, not least because of the novel mode of transport (yes, it's fun, and better than an elephant ride), but above all because the vehicle's movement at moderate speed stirs up a cooling breeze, extremely welcome in the great heat and humidity. From Siem Reap you approach the vast archaeological park lying several miles to the north. After passing through the inconspicuous first entrance, you still must go some real distance to reach the second entrance, the main gate, a control point, an elaborate structure with separate functions, including multiple ticket windows. You cannot pass without buying a ticket.

In Cambodia and Thailand at least, soldiers function not just as guards but as service people, a neat and convenient system. Here you can buy a pass for a day, or several days, or for a week. (Anent the latter you pick the days that you want to visit whether one after another,

1, 2, 3, 4, etc., or spread out as you wish.) At $20.00 for a single day per person, the seven-day pass at $60.00 represents a genuine savings, even if you do not use it for the full allotment of time. My pass began on Monday, 15 March, and expired on Tuesday, 13 April. As it resulted, I used my pass for only five days overall. Any linear measurements that I mention are only approximations, translating from kilometers or simple meters, and I use them only to give the reader some kind of rough idea.

ANGKOR WAT, Monday, 15 March 2010, a day that shall abide in my memory forever. Bombarded by vendors on arriving at this unique and sublime edifice (dedicated to Vishnu), I quickly but firmly shook them off. Mounting the causeway and heading east to the western and chief entrance (the southern portal of which shelters a beautiful statue of Vishnu), I crossed the moat that measures some 600 feet wide. Even without the moat, the temple compound makes quite a large rectangle. The temple with the moat equals about one square mile. For a just comparison, remember that the original walled-in Roman London (on the northern side of the Thames), the present so-called City of London (the heart of the British capital), covers about one square mile.

Despite the later Buddhist additions, Angkor Wat remains one of Hinduism's most powerful architectural statements, albeit created in Cambodia. As in all such statements, the apparent contradiction (a true paradox), of reason versus faith, of the rational versus the irrational, struck me yet all over again. Someone, some leader, had commanded vast resources to have others build in a highly logical manner (construction in stone on this scale demands rigorous organization, discipline, and logic) a huge structure absolutely embodying the expression of the otherworldly. Brahmanic or Buddhist, Buddha himself became added to the Hindu cosmogony and pantheon, a result that he did not intend. This led me to ponder that older Trinity that goes back to around 4000 B.C.E., Brahma the Creator, Vishnu the Preserver, and Shiva the Destroyer, thus preceding the Christian Trinity literally by some four millennia.

Once I reached the main entrance on the west with its three portals, rather than entering there, I veered north; and staying in the shade of any and all trees as much as possible, I walked around the whole northern half of the temple outside the non-defensive wall, going to the temple's limit on the east. Then backtracking to the eastern entrance, I rested in the shade of a grove of trees to the southwest of that gateway. Here I had the unexpected pleasure of sitting near, and conversing in French with, a young-looking and only recently retired couple from Paris (Annie and André). Finally I made my entrance into the immense temple compound itself, circulating mainly inside the northern half while generally advancing west.

The scope, the beauty, and the sculptural detail I found simply overwhelming, and the experience willy-nilly became a religious one. From aesthetics it passed to the divine. My eyes kept filling with tears of amazement, wonder, and even piety. I did not ascend on this occasion to the temple's third and highest level (saving that for another visit), but did walk around the second level, as well as (of course) the first or main level. By now the heat had become so pronounced that I called it a day. As I exited the western entrance, I rendered homage to the eight-armed statue of Vishnu. I returned to the vendors' area, bought a few souvenirs, sought and found Hong and his tuk-tuk, got us each a cool drink, and then retreated to Siem Reap and the cool oasis of my fancy hotel.

Once back in my chamber's private space, completely overcome by my combined aesthetic and religious experience, I burst into tears and even sobs. The depth of my reaction astonished me. Once I recovered from this catharsis, I did my daily exercises, and after showering, I went at once for a prolonged swim. Returning to my chamber, I ate a small snack, drank more water, took a nap for several hours, and did not venture forth again until the early evening and my meal in the main part of Siem Reap, courtesy of Hong and his trusty tuk-tuk. That night of nights following that day of days, I specifically patronized the restaurant Happy Herb Pizza, where I ate a medium-sized "happy herb" pizza (a small would have sufficed), saving a few pieces for later. This especial item on the menu totally lived up to its name, containing as it did what seemed like some excellent ganja as the herb of choice. Need I add that I slept marvelously well that night? It became the perfect end of a truly amazing day. As I fell asleep, I pondered on the depth, wisdom, and resonance of Hinduism, the world's oldest religion.

Tuesday, 16 March. My plans for today, to visit Angkor Thom, became sidetracked. Hong wanted me to go out to Angkor to see the sunset over Angkor Wat to the southeast of Phnom Bakheng (not far to the southwest of Angkor Thom's great south gate), from the top of that temple-mountain (the first one built in the Angkor area after Roluos) that sits in turn upon a large, free-standing hill or small mountain, something that the guidebooks do not make very clear. Instead, his plan not working out (I did not want to go out there in the evening), we made a tour (for the same price), my first, of Siem Reap, which I had planned to visit anyway, and more than once. I far prefer Siem Reap to Phnom Penh, less crowded and much more fun, what with all the hedonistic young people flocking to the small city. Also, Hong was having some family problems, and before returning to my hotel we finished up our little tour by visiting his family at their home, humble but adequate. Their toilet was a communal one (three or four toilets to one side in the shade), but their home had the basics, running water, a medium-sized TV, a small fridge, etc.

His wife keeps the kids and the house scrupulously clean, I could not help noticing. We all went shopping, ending up at a much cheaper covered market (where the natives go), and his wife Thé (a warm and practical woman) helped me buy a new pair of short trousers (down to the knees) and a new long-sleeved shirt of cotton (much cooler than synthetic fabric). Not anticipating the great heat so soon, I had not brought with me enough light-weight clothes, and had been forced to wear the same shorts and shirt over and over, washing them at night and letting them dry out by morning. Although some tourists might have objected to losing the day (or so it seemed) to an unknown family, I did not, even if quite frankly I felt uneasy when I noted in what poverty Hong's family lived. As I had informed him at the start, I could only help by hiring his tuk-tuk service, well, for the most part. That evening when we parted after my evening meal in Siem Reap (I ate at Ecstatic Pizza, but in that special way [no marijuana] it could not compete with Happy Herb Pizza, although as pizza goes it's okay), I gave Hong some extra money to help him out. Tomorrow we shall go to Angkor Thom to visit the main monuments in the middle of that great urban space.

Wednesday, 17 March. Another surprising and even astonishing day! It also turned out as one of my costliest occasions as well. Without further delay Hong now took me past Angkor Wat, and then through the picturesque south gate, on into Angkor Thom, an enormous urban space inside its far-reaching walls, wider east and west than north and south. A word about the four or five major gates of this big town. Like the temple entrances, the builders located the four major gates according to the four major compass points, and then added the Victory Gate north of the east gate. (North and south gates are open, but east and west are closed. The Victory Gate serves as the de facto east gate.) The Khmers built the temples and other related structures out of stone (laterite, brick, etc.), but all other edifices out of wood in a similar architectural style. They have all gone, and the urban space inside the walls lies empty, apart from the temples, etc. More on these monuments later.

Today I visited at the urban core the Bayon, the Baphuon, a corner of the former palace compound, the *Terrasse aux éléphants,* the separate Terrace of the Leper King, walking in and around these and other structures. An especial height measured from the ground that one perceives over and over on all the buildings: that from these vantage points the individual could easily mount onto the back of an elephant. Hardly any locale exists where elephants can or could not go, and once they must have flooded the main streets and plazas, as ubiquitous as horses in the West before gasoline-powered vehicles. Following my visit to the above locales, Hong next took me to Ta Prohm, the famous jungle-entangled temple purposely kept that way for tourists. By this time I had walked enough, albeit mostly in the shade, and I had seen enough, at least for that day. We decided to head back to the hotel in Siem Reap.

As it emerged, I had not been drinking enough water whether in Phnom Penh, or Siem Reap, or Angkor. I had been taking vitamins and other supplements every day, but my body must have lost essential salts and minerals. The lack of enough water caught up with me. Late that afternoon I went down to the front desk (I happened to have my shoulder bag on me with essentials) for something, and as I walked away, I fainted and fell, but sans injury. A young man on the staff took me to the nearest (small) emergency clinic not far away; there the doctor on duty diagnosed a touch of dysentery, plus the main culprit, the insufficiency of water. He soon had me almost back to normal, and gave me vitamin and mineral packets to take over several days, recommending rest for a day or so, staying out of the sun, etc. I followed his advice and recovered in record time—in fact, by Friday. I got word to Hong that night not to pick me up (I would eat in the hotel), nor in the morning. I would take a day off, and rest and recuperate in the hotel.

This experience points up the fact that, when traveling (especially to exotic locales), other factors can come into play besides what places one chooses to visit and how long one spends in them! Now, back to the monuments that I visited earlier that Wednesday, a subject of much greater interest to me than my own minor health issues, once I had addressed them (to the tune of $65.00). Even allowing that Cambodian tuk-tuks function best at moderate speed and that they can easily reach that velocity, it requires some real time to go from Angkor Thom's south gate to its urban center, not quite in the geographical middle, to see the monuments congregated there.

First, the Bayon—what an incredible structure! As often remarked, it looks like a pile of rubble from a distance, an effect enhanced by the orange and yellow lichens that flourish on the temple's fifty-four incredible towers, each with the four Buddha-like, impassively smiling faces directed to the compass's four cardinal points. Once you approach and then enter the edifice, these gigantic faces glare down at you, or so it seems, from every angle, and as you ascend into the interior, sometimes at almost your own eye level. The Bayon is the greatest piece of fantastic architecture that I have ever experienced. It stirs up such a mixture of conflicting emotions, awe, fright, wonder, love, admiration, etc., and it remains the greatest example of what I call Khmer or Angkor Baroque. What a feast for the eye!

Second, the Baphuon—another spectacular site, a true temple-mountain! The EFEO had by 1970 dismantled the building, and had laid all the pieces out all around on the earth like a gigantic jigsaw puzzle, when the civil broke out. Then under the Khmer Rouge regime the records (extant only in Cambodia, but utterly needed to put all the pieces together) somehow became destroyed (not intentionally), a real disaster for the archaeologists. Luckily, back in Paris sufficient photos existed so that the people in charge could use them, in addition to computers, to put the building back in place. The work began in 1995 and should terminate later this year or in 2011, a tremendous task.

I walked up to the structure, but could only guess at its awesome size. The building itself stands shrouded in plastic-sheeted scaffolding, permitting no real visual examination. We discuss here only the major structures, but many other buildings exist all around the major ones, these others perhaps minor but no less fascinating. The very long and high-sitting Elephant Terrace, and the lesser but quite interesting Terrace of the so-called Leper King, would have served as the major focus for elephant-borne transport, whether for mounting or dismounting. These monuments mostly stand on the west of the city's main plaza, going from south to north, and face the twelve laterite towers collectively known as Prasat Suor Prat; these rise up on the plaza's eastern edge.

Thursday, 18 March. Per doctor's orders I rested much of this day, remaining where it was cool, reading, drinking a lot of water, exercising, swimming, eating, napping. Despite all the repose I still managed to sleep well that night. All this rest did me a lot of good, and I had much recuperated by breakfast the next day. Friday morning found me somewhat restless (the usual too much energy) and eager to return to Angkor.

Friday, 19 March. As usual, we left the hotel at 8:30 A.M. and returned at 12:30 P.M. I contented myself with visiting only two sites, and at great leisure: first, Phnom Bakheng, located just a little southwest of Angkor Thom's imposing south gate; and then, second, Preah Khan, located northeast of the northeast corner of Angkor Thom and, as an overall site, only a little bit less large than Angkor Wat inside its moat.

After Hong left me at the entrance to Phnom Bakheng (which rises amid a new-growth tropical forest), I had to hike some real distance to reach the base (facing east) of the little free-standing, forested mountain upon which sits the temple itself. No one was around, and the elephant ride to the top had not yet begun for the day. I took the trail on the right for pedestrians that goes up and around the big hill at an easy angle of ascent. A very nice promenade indeed.

However, despite the sign forbidding it, "the imp of the perverse" (to use Poe's elegant phrase) almost made me take the left-hand path that the elephants use. Although I probably could have negotiated it, the condition of that track—doubtlessly littered here and there by large piles of elephant excrement (possibly awkward to pass)—suddenly flashed into my mind and made me continue my hike up the right-hand track, ahem!

The easy ascent makes an ideal walk for folk not accustomed to climbing a hill or small mountain. Unexpected vistas of the surrounding countryside open up here and there through the hillside foliage. Slightly extending out over the hillside, an occasional wooden deck with benches (often in the shade) will come into view. In these niches one can sit and hang out and rest.

Once on the mountain top one can clearly observe how the ancient Khmers, to make this temple-mountain, leveled the summit down to the bedrock, leaving a pyramid of stone that they then cut into terraces and steps, yet further sculpting it. They thus carved the temple core out of the rock but built other smaller structures (as part of the temple) out of rock or brick. The stone, black with age, presents a somber spectacle indeed in the morning sunlight. The central staircases on each of the four sides orient as usual to the four cardinal compass points. The ancient Khmers had a genius for precision!

Guarded by stylized lions and little towers, the steep stairs take real care to negotiate the climb to the top of the temple-mountain. The visitor (or should I not say the pilgrim?) finds a genuine reward in the cooling breezes there, as well as in the views of Angkor Wat on the southeast, no less than those of the enormous Western Baray to the direct west of Angkor Thom—but not those of the only a little less enormous Eastern Baray, not at all visible from this peak. These reservoirs must have held an enormous quantity of rainy-season water provided by the Mekong river. The visitor also notices what a good job the modern Khmers have done clearing the temple of tropical verdure. The workers one sees mostly on the spacious mid-terrace patiently toil at restoring the temple where needed here and there.

After walking around the temple-mountain (what a delight all these little towers and turrets provide for the eye!), climbing it, lingering there at the summit to take in the wonderful panoramas laid out all around, and then descending at last from that unique high point;—I then went back down the regular trail (not that used one for the elephant ride!), and just as I had met a few people on the way up, I now met a few others on the way down. Once I reached the ground, I hiked back through the forest and then the entrance near the access road to Angkor Thom, where I found Hong awaiting my return. I probably spent a good couple of hours at this locale. Minus the usual crowds (especially at sunset), the place provided me with the most satisfying experience I had at Angkor overall, that is, apart from Angkor Wat. If ever I come back here, I'll take the elephant ride to the top and then back down!

An important aside here, as occasioned by my recollection of the workers patiently toiling at Phnom Bakheng. I may have failed so far to emphasize enough the marvelously humane cheerfulness not just of the people in Thailand but especially of the people in Cambodia, where more than a little gallantry, a certain resolute bravery, comes into play. The modern Khmers have gone through hell and back during the long years of civil war (1970-98), but above all under the Khmer Rouge (1975-79). Nobody who has lived through something like that can ever forget it, and while they may have learned of it from surviving parents and grandparents, the younger generation symbolizes a kind of triumph over adversity.

As waged mostly by the Americans, the Vietnam War served as both catalyst and then as prolongation of all the death and suffering that happened in Cambodia. Thus I can perceive how the present-day Khmers remain as great in their own original manner as their ancestors who created these incredible and fantasticated monuments. Any people who can survive the hell that the Cambodians did remain a great people. In a certain sense the worship of the old Indic pantheon has not died out in Southeast Asia, whether Brahma, Vishnu, Shiva, or Buddha. It still exerts a real presence (that is, beyond contemporary Buddhism) and aesthetically captures or captivates visitors or pilgrims from far away who come with very different religious backgrounds. That is for sure something to ponder. I salute the good cheer and gallantry of the Khmer people!

Hong took me to Preah Khan. Earlier, in comparing this place to Angkor Wat, I stated that it measured overall a little bit less large. That needs emendation. Angkor Wat measures 332 by 258 meters, and Preah Khan 200 by 175—strictly comparing temple precincts alone—and thus overall Preah Khan comes out about one-third smaller than Angkor Wat. Nonetheless, at merely two-thirds the size of the larger temple (the largest religious edifice in the world), the smaller one still remains very large indeed. It takes rank as both a temple and a Buddhist university that once harbored more than a thousand professors. Although relatively free of jungle entanglements, great pieces of the architectural fabric have fallen down and extend in great confusion outside the main inner passageway, given the complicated floor plan of multiple chambers in the central mass running east and west. The central passage running through the middle of the three chief masses remains clear and easy to traverse, and moreover almost completely in the shade, an important condition for me following Phnom Bakheng, and walking around in the sun at the summit of both the hill and the temple, even with minimal garb and béret.

To reach Preah Khan, we passed through the great north gate of Angkor Thom after entering through the great south portal. The distance across the town (a giant walled square) takes time to cover in a tuk-tuk and impresses the visitor with the sheer size of the city layout. In turn, the sheer size and complexity of the temple-university's layout also stunned me. Hong left me off at the west entrance, and so I traversed the accessible inner passage west to east, but returning east to west, I tried going along the northern (verdured) part of the compound, but the rocky chaos (created by all the masonry fallen down) forced me back inside, to continue my return traversal of the inner passage. I hardly spent an hour at Preah Khan, but going there and returning through Angkor Thom required more time than anticipated. It had already become quite hot. By noon I called it a day, and at my urgent request Hong brought me back to the hotel around 12:30. As usual, I enjoyed the fresh breezy ride back to Siem Reap. I can't quite recall where I ate that night, probably at Molly Malone's in central Siem Reap, rather a fun bar serving Anglo-Irish fare, fish and chips, pasties, Guinness, etc. Despite the Cambodian servers, etc., the place retained a genuinely Hibernian feel.

(An aside. Sometime early during my stay at the Monoreach Hotel, probably Tuesday, 16 March, I phoned my friend Stan Guyuski, who lives at the resort that he runs on Koh Samui, to tell him that I would be coming down to visit him around Friday, 26 March, after I returned from Cambodia, staying again at the Swan Hotel during 24 and 25 March. I had already phoned him once, from Bangkok, after I had landed, to let him know that I had actually arrived in Thailand.)

Saturday, 20 March. By this date I had become rather templed out. Still, on my seven-day pass I had a few more days to go—waste not, want not—and so I decided to visit Angkor on Saturday and Monday, taking a break on Sunday to visit Siem Reap again. On Saturday we concentrated on sites at and around Angkor Thom's de facto eastern portal, the Victory Gate. I contented myself by mostly walking around the various temples, and then entering them briefly with no particular plan. Here are the chief sites visited. Just outside the gate (across the east-west road from each other), the Thommanon on the north and Chau Say Tevoda on the south (very similar to each other), the first beautifully restored, the second in ruins awaiting restoration. Further east from Chau Say Tevoda, the gigantic but unfinished Ta Keo (unfinished meaning undecorated) with the summit of its chief tower almost reaching 150 feet, all quite imposing.

From these temples we went east past the already visited but ever impressive Ta Prohm, and reaching the massive and atmospheric ruins of Banteay Kdei (once a Buddhist monastery), we turned right, going south until we arrived at my favorite shrine for that day, Prasat Kravan, the sanctuary dedicated to Vishnu like Angkor Wat, nothing immense for a change but in fact a much smaller temple, of choice design and elegant make, lovingly restored. Constructed of pale yellow brick, it consists of five towers (the central one the highest), unusually laid out in a row north and south, all on the same narrow low terrace or platform. Inside the central and northern towers (on the three walls not including those with the east-facing doors), some unique and striking bas-reliefs, carved out of the brick walls, depict Vishnu as well as his consort Lakshmi, respectively. After so much colossal architecture this place made a delightful and refreshing contrast.

Facing east in the usual way, the shrine stood in the full sunlight. Any shade fell only under the few trees growing on the margin of the temple's clearing. By high noon I was feeling the great heat and asked Hong to return me to my hotel sans delay. Bidding adieu to this exquisite shrine, we headed southwest, following the access road on toward Angkor Wat, then going west along the southeast corner of that temple's immense moat, exiting out the main road leading past the Angkor Ticket Checkpoint and then finally back to Siem Reap. Approaching it initially from a different (unknown) angle, I did not recognize the gigantic moat at once, but perceived it as a large lake! As I returned to my hotel, no natural breeze could have proven more welcome than that stirred up by the movement of Hong's tuk-tuk.

That night I had Hong take me to the Red Piano (Bar) Restaurant in town, a handsomely restored colonial house on the northeast corner of an intersection near Molly Malone's a bit further to the west. Instead of sitting at a table on the balcony upstairs, I opted for a table downstairs, not right on the street but set back a bit inside a secure little corner of the southern verandah. As usual, I ordered fish, this time with rice and veggies, along with several drinks with rum, including an Angelina Jolie named after the actress who dined here on several occasions. It's a purty good cocktail! (She was making a movie nearby.)

Sunday, 21 March. A blessèdly quiet and uneventful day in Siem Reap far from crowds and vendors at archaeological sites. We got going early and finished early. Hong took me around to several bookstores, which also sell inexpensive but attractive souvenirs. I picked up a few items, including a CD of traditional Khmer folk music. We visited with Hong's entire nuclear family again, and again this proved a warm and enjoyable time. I didn't care to dawdle, and as soon as possible (without my being impolite) we left, and I had Hong take me to the large and beautifully laid out arts-and-crafts high-quality store, the Artisans d'Angkor—just southwest of the main bar-and-restaurant area that I had been patronizing since my arrival in Siem Reap—where I had planned to buy a bunch of small but elegant souvenirs for friends, and where the Chantiers Écoles (workshop schools) sell their products ranging from furniture and household items to nifty decorative items whether made out of stone, wood, or metal.

These workshops teach various handicrafts to impoverished young people, thus giving them the chance at a professional trade, and thus helping to revive some important traditional Cambodian culture. The store swarmed with customers while I was rambling about, inspecting the goods for sale. At the last minute I decided not to buy anything, electing to give the $50.00 (bill) that I had put aside for purchases at this place to Hong himself as a worthy tip at the last minute on the last day that he worked for me; it seemed to me that I could effect much more good by giving the sum to a Cambodian (and his family) whom I knew personally rather than to a worthwhile institution, none of whose people I had so much as met. Hong was not less deserving. Besides, the store appeared to be doing a prodigious business.

That evening I ate at the two-story Funky Munky, indeed a "great little bar-restaurant" (to quote the Lonely Planet guide), celebrated for its alcoholic beverages and its hamburgers that the customer can have made exactly to a specific preference. Seeing no one (clients or waiters) in the little downstairs with tables and chairs open to the street, I mounted the staircase inside at the back and found on the second level a much larger space with a big balcony overlooking the street. People were sitting at tables here and there, drinking, eating, and hanging out, always the good sign of a great eatery-cum-bar. Altogether, a mellow place! I sat at a table close to the balcony and ordered a regular cheeseburger but with blue cheese, as well as French fries and a mai tai.

Everything came out excellent: cheeseburger scrumptious, French fries authentic chips English-style, and the mai tai so delicious, exceptional (with fresh coconut milk), and generous that no sooner had I guzzled it down than I got up and ordered a second one directly at the bar behind me toward the back. I complimented the bartender on duty about the drink and food; he turned out to be the owner himself, who had come from London and had set up this great little place. I told him that the mai tai was the best that I had ever drunk, and ordered another one. He smiled and laughed, and we talked a little before I went back to my table to await my alcoholic dessert. (The service was casual but cheerful and prompt.) After I paid the bill and lingered a bit longer, Hong took me back to my fancy hotel.

Monday, 22 March. Well, I had come to my final day at Angkor, and I absolutely could not think of a better place to visit, or to visit again, than that Mother of All Temples, Angkor Wat herself. Even if I had been going past the temple one way or another most of the week, it had not lost any of its allure, mystique, or enigma. By enigma I don't mean the lack of any historical or archaeological data. We now know quite a bit about the history of Angkor and the Khmer

Empire. By enigma I mean this: that all old structures, hoary with age, of whatever provenience (which have survived more or less intact), possess an essence that has deepened and accrued over the centuries or millennia. This essence is what we as human beings feel or sense in an unique way—at once a religious and aesthetic response—an essence that allures us with an eternal fascination, and never to be exhausted.

When Hong dropped me off near the outer (western) entrance to Angkor Wat, I crossed the extensive moat on the great sandstone causeway. This time I entered through the portal on the left (the central one still undergoes repair) and proceeded all the way to the eastern entrance, a little hike that took a little while. Out of necessity I passed around the three stories or terraces of the central temple complex. I then backtracked up onto the first story, then the second, and last the third one (something that I had not done my first visit) through the very steep but safe wooden stairs at the northeast corner, much easier to climb than the quite awkward (original) stone stairs. I walked in and around the galleries on this top terrace (great views and a cooling breeze); and as I had climbed from terrace to terrace, I had loitered at each successive level, mostly in the shade, and I loitered at the third and last level the longest.

Moreover, I had once again brought with me a bottle of water, from which I would imbibe on occasion. I had learned my lesson from that past Wednesday! Looking out from the central southern "window" of the gallery on that side of the top terrace, I noted again the much smaller modern temple sited in the middle of that richly verdured expanse on the south (the outbuildings evidently house the monks who serve this temple), and then to the east of it the little thatched and wooden village where some rare local people reside, the modest buildings as usual raised up on stilts. As the last part of this my last pilgrimage to the Mother of All Temples, I decided to explore a little of that whole southern half of Angkor Wat's terrain, as walled in by the moat. I descended, and going past the modern temple and village, I exited the great south gate, which features yet another active shrine, tended by some youngsters.

From this point I walked east between moat and wall to the great southeast corner, and next I turned a sharp left to the north, which led me to the great east gate. There I entered, by means of some access roads I passed through the wooded region of the immense southeastern sector, that is, to the southeast of the central temple complex. Eventually I walked again the same road that I had taken to go from that complex to and through the great south gate. All this hiking I did as much as possible in the shade effected by the morning sunlight upon the foliage of the numerous trees. The great heat did not seem to bother me much that day, probably because of the slight overcast. Presently I hiked west between moat and wall until I reached the great southwest corner, where I turned sharply north, continuing between moat and wall.

As I came abreast of the southern portal of the central entrance, the great west gate, I noted with surprise the absence of anyone at all in the chamber housing Vishnu. This encouraged me to approach and to pay my devoirs, as a son to a father. Raising my hands to my forehead in the prayer salute (fingers pointing upwards), I bowed in respect and wonder to the handsome statue. I must have unconsciously addressed a prayer to Vishnu, because late that afternoon Vishnu answered it. It gave me one of the most unusual sensations that I have ever had in my life so far. I say no more about it. What happened will remain private. I realized then and later that in the course of this last visit circumstances had allowed me many exceptional moments in private, undisturbed by other visitors. The moment with Vishnu had come unbidden (or so I thought) but was not ungratefully received.

Returning across the great sandstone causeway, I hiked back into the outer world. I turned around to take a last look, a prolonged look, at the great (and unforgettable) triple western entrance across the waters of the vast moat. Searching here and there, I finally found Hong in the location where many tuk-tuk drivers park while waiting for their riders to return from the temple. There in the shade Hong had been catching much-needed slumber in the back of his vehicle. Once more, and now for the last time, we headed back from Angkor to the Monoreach Hotel, where he would pick me again in the evening for my meal in central Siem Reap.

That night I had Hong take me back to the first restaurant, to the first eatery where I had gone, Happy Herb (or Herb's) Pizza (an offshoot of the original in Phnom Penh). Only this time I ordered only a small "happy herb" special. The small pizza made its due appearance, nicely sliced, and as I ate it, I washed it down with several cans of a good local stout. When Hong dropped me off back at my hotel, we arranged for him to take me to the bus station (primarily a parking lot) where I would board the air-conditioned bus back to Phnom Penh the following day, Tuesday, 23 March. As we parted that night, I gave him the $50 bill that I had saved for him, the equivalent of his working for me during three days involving the little tour or small circuit at $16 per occasion, as opposed to $20 for the extended tour or big circuit per occasion. In the dark he could not notice the bill's high denomination (high by Cambodian standards), but in the morning when he came to pick me up, Hong definitely let me know that he had indeed noticed. It made me feel good.

Imagine my surprise the next day, when Hong came to get me after mid-morning, to find his friend Pisay (who works in the hotel restaurant) driving the tuk-tuk, with Hong and his family somehow tucked into the two-wheel carriage! Pisay drove so Hong could converse with me. They were all giving me a great big family send-off! The family somehow found room for me and my baggage. They all hung out at the bus station until I boarded my late-morning bus. We all gave each other a great big hug. A nice fuzzy feeling!

After another night at the Hotel Cara back in Phnom Penh, I flew back to Bangkok on 24 March, overnighting there on both the 24th and the 25th, once again at the Swan Hotel. At the start of this account I refer to it as a "little report," and it has exceeded already by half what I purposed to write. A brief summary can suffice for the rest. On Friday the 26th, I took the Lomphrayah bus-and-boat combo to the island of Koh Samui, the air-conditioned and toilet-equipped bus to Chumphon facing east from the Thai-Malay peninsula, and then the huge catamaran speed boat to the several islands that terminate in the good-sized expanse of Koh Samui.

There at bamboo-enshrouded Baan Shadis Samui, just inland of Mae Nam on the north central coast, where he rents out villas, I passed an idyllic two and a half weeks with my great and good friend Stan Guyuski. Koh Samui, with its unique mix of local Thai and outlanders from everywhere (but especially from the ubiquitous Anglophone world), must rank as the closest place to paradise or utopia that I have ever had the pleasure to visit while incarnated in human form. Thanks to Stan I had no hotel bills, and we ate our meals out at great little eateries at little cost (one to three dollars on average). When Stan was not attending to his resort chores (I helped keep the leaves and things out of the swimming pool), we occupied ourselves with talking, reading, and listening to music. This halcyonic existence came to an end for me on 12 April. Koh Samui is a large and very beautiful tropical island kept cool by ocean breezes.

I effected my return to Bangkok via several stages—first by the local ferry to Surat Thani on the afternoon of 12 April, then the evening train (leaving around 5:30 P.M.) during the night of 12-13, arriving in the very early morning, when a taximeter promptly got me back to the Swan Hotel. There I overnighted once again during 13-14-15. I had returned to a very quiet city, apart from the Red Shirt protesters carrying on at some distance from my hotel. Quiet mostly reigned on those three dates: the Thai New Year was taking place, and most shops and restaurants had closed. At long last I flew home (a pleasant routine flight) on 16 April via China Air Lines, which had taken me all the way to Bangkok during 28 February and 1-2 March. An excellent airline, by the way. I reached Los Angeles via LAX by mid-evening, and I arrived home by taxi soon after. Overall, an unprecedented voyage for me, my first such trip overall to Asia. A very special and very big thanks to my friend Stan, not just a wonderful host but a great all-around companion. Blessed with a brilliant and keenly enquiring mind, he remains one of the best-read and best-informed people whom I know.

A Sentimental Pilgrimage to Mother Egypt

a poet's impressions

DEDICATION AND ACKNOWLEDGMENTS

This account of a recent voyage to Egypt I dedicate to a variety of friends whose financial or whose practical assistance helped make it possible: first, Linda and Tim McKenna, Derrick Hussey (my current publisher), and above all Leo Grin for arranging my air flights to and from Egypt, and for contacting the Luna Hotel and the tourist liaison there, Abdou (Hany Mohamed); second, Robin R. Reynolds III, Michael and Renée Halverson, and Stanley C. Sargent, the consulting Egyptologist for our Weird Con(vention) group largely located in Northern California; third, in a class by himself, Abdou, who works for and out of the Luna Hotel in downtown Cairo, not far from the nonpareil Egyptian Museum or (for that matter) Tahrir Square (generally to be avoided), where determined protesters have encamped.

Thanks to Abdou (pronounced ab-DOU) and his network of friends and collaborators throughout Lower and Upper Egypt (that is, northern and southern Egypt), and thanks to the miracle of portable telephones, I traveled calm and comfortable from Cairo in the north all the way down south to Abu Simbel and back. Abdou is a professional driver, practical guide, and travel agent working with other travel agents. You do not engage with Ancient Egypt unless you first engage with Modern Egypt, upon which you totally depend: they speak English, but generally as a tourist you do not speak Arabic! Abdou arranged my personal itinerary almost on an ad hoc basis, once I arrived in Egypt. His telephone number is: (+20) 1000088578. My personal indebtedness to Abdou and his collaborators while I travelled in Egypt remains absolutely paramount. I express here my profound gratitude and appreciation to all of them.

—Donald Sidney-Fryer

Westchester, Los Angeles,
California, March 2013.

PREFACE-WARNING

Unless you travel in remote areas away from big cities, and unless you are crazy, determined, and young, you do not backpack in Egypt, or unless you are with a group and guide. You will be at risk, especially a woman, even if with a man. Camp out in budget hotels, where you have a maximum of quiet and protection.

Also, unless you have something of the local idiom, find yourself in a rustic or remote area, and are accustomed to the conditions of driving in the Third World (especially in the big cities), you don't drive in a country like Egypt or Thailand or Cambodia. People seem to drive in almost every direction while ostensibly going one of two ways. Few traffic lights exist, maybe a few traffic officers might be directing traffic at an intersection, usually problematical. Meanwhile pedestrians dart in and out of traffic, threading their way amid the vehicles. Almost no accidents appear to happen (I saw none in any of these countries), but for a person coming from the First World the traffic seems like pure chaos, at once dangerous and frightening. Beware!

A Sentimental Pilgrimage to Mother Egypt

In explanation of my title, I must say that the sentiment or sentimentality (used here simply to denote pure human emotion), as mixed in with a preeminent sense of latent wonder or marvel, does not come cheaply. Even if done as frugally as possible (maybe not the best option), travel is expensive. Much preliminary thought and care, many tentative plans, and then overt flexibility come into play, to make up any jaunt in another country, especially one that belongs culturally to the Middle East, where the Islamic religion dominates.

Journeying to and from a given country, staying overnight in hotels, eating in hotels or nearby restaurants—all this does not come cheaply. Although I set up my itinerary with an independent entrepreneur in Cairo, once I arrived in Egypt and had settled in at my hotel—in my case it worked, and it worked very well, thanks to the driver-agent-guide—I now grasp why most people choose a package tour as arranged by an American travel agent in the United States working with a native travel agent in Egypt.

As an added factor, and moreover as part of the cost in a country like Egypt, tipping is essential, if not obligatory. Service people in hotels and at special sites don't earn that much, and therefore they rely on tips for a major part of their income. Don't tip, or don't tip much, if the service is poor, but overall be compassionate: tip appropriately. Since I rarely tip in my own country (except in restaurants), learning how to tip became for me personally quite an ordeal or struggle. However, I think that I did finally get the hang of it thanks to my patient guides and drivers. You can download a guide off the Internet on how to tip in Egypt: it is basically hierarchical according to the type or level of service received. You must often visit nearby banks to make sure that you have enough one-pound coins, five-pound and/or ten-pound notes (bills), as the situation may demand.

A special injunction. Unless you form part of an especial tour group traveling from hotel to ancient site by bus and then back—and often traveling with some kind of group is impossible to avoid, nor is it desirable to avoid it—you can arrange to travel anywhere out of your hotel and then back, independently, with your own driver and (Egyptological) guide. This is what I did, and this will save the tourist from much bother and from being pestered at the given site, from local people offering their services or souvenirs. The simple presence of your own guide accompanying you usually serves to keep you unmolested. And you must learn to say no or simply to ignore importunate people, something that I find initially hard to do.

One further piece of advice. If you go to Egypt, then go with someone, a close friend, a special companion, a marriage partner. At its best, voyaging with someone compatible does indeed amplify, does probably double, the pleasure and excitement when visiting extraordinary historical and/or archaeological sites. Although I usually enjoy traveling solo, my trip to Egypt would have turned out even more enjoyable had I gone in the company of some special friend.

The big question: why go to Egypt? Especially to Mother Egypt, as in Mother India or Mother Africa? Like many other people, I became fascinated by Ancient Egypt in my youth, and in my case while in the fourth grade of elementary school (Mt. Pleasant Grammar School, New Bedford, Massachusetts), when first studying geography with Miss O'Malley during the winter of 1943-44 (the Japanese had surprise-bombed Pearl Harbor on 7 December 1941). I was discovering how big and various and beautiful our planet Earth still remained. An illustration in some Book of Knowledge, a piece of nineteenth-century art (a color painting reproduced in black and white) depicting a landscape in Ancient Egypt: what captured my attention and captivated my imagination—beyond the curious obelisks and palm trees—was that the central feature represented an army of peasants pulling to the left from the right a giant black sphinx on an equally large wooden platform with multiple wheels. One or more pyramids also appeared in the background, adding to the mystery.

What antique land was this that could give birth to such an exotic phenomenon as the one depicted in this tableau?! From that time onward I kept a lookout, more desultory than purposeful, for stories and articles in books and periodicals dealing with Ancient and Modern Egypt, especially in the ever enlightening and innovative *National Geographic* magazine. Later on I learned that Giuseppe Verdi had created a grand opera laid in Ancient Egypt, *Aida,* for the opening of the Suez Canal in 1871. And still somewhat after that, I learned that the ballet master Marius Petipa had scored his first colossal success with a massive and majestic ballet d'action, at St. Petersburg in 1862, *Pharaoh's Daughter,* the first opus on the stage anywhere to bring Ancient Egypt to life in a major and certainly lavish way.

Then about two years ago, thanks to correspondence with Egyptologist friend Stan Sargent in San Francisco, my interest in Ancient Egypt became reignited, and I began reading and re-reading many books on Egypt, many borrowed from UCLA's incomparable Research Library (and Annex), some generously given me by various friends, Stan himself supplying the excellent general text *The Egyptians* by Cyril Aldred and Aidan Dodson, and Leo Grin furnishing the latest edition of *The Oxford History of Ancient Egypt.* On my own I found and read *The Cambridge History of Islamic Egypt,* to help me grasp both Islamic and Modern Egypt. Finally, but finally, I decided that I had to visit Egypt before I left my current incarnation. But I had almost visited the Land of the Nile in the winter of 2010-11. Instead, I had opted at that time to visit another but similar locale, all proportions guarded.

In the winter of 2010-11 I sojourned for not quite two months in Southeast Asia, meaning Thailand and Cambodia, primarily to visit Angkor, the chief center of the once great Khmer Empire and civilization. I had long since remarked the affinities between Ancient Egypt and not so ancient Cambodia, but in the difficult choice between the two countries (as to which one to visit first) I chose Cambodia via the gateway metropolis of Bangkok, the capital of Thailand, as most outlanders do. Having survived the Khmer Rouge régime of 1975-79, and having recovered as much as possible from the negative effects of that regime, the new modern Cambodia that has come into existence has done so thus only some five centuries after Siam had captured and looted Angkor in 1431.

The modern Cambodians still speak essentially the same language as their illustrious forebears and remain that much closer than the modern Egyptians to their much remoter ancestors. Moreover, apart from the Coptic (ancient Egyptian plus Greek) featured in the liturgy of the Coptic Church, modern Egypt speaks Arabic as its chief language (followed closely by English, the new international lingua franca), and no longer uses its own original tongue for everyday transactions, a crucial difference.

Now, finally, it had become Egypt's turn for my long-desired and long-delayed sojourn there. I not only read much and in depth but, strategically, I began saving my shekels from here and there (earnings from my publishers, no less than from my sales of my own books at readings and signings). Beneficent and benevolent friends began donating sums both large and small to my Egypt safari fund—may the blessings of Amun-Ra descend upon them all! Slowly, deliberately, I saved as much as I could, and once I reached the total of more than $5100, late in 2012, then the time had come to plan and arrange my trip by means of my computer expert friend Leo Grin. I waited until after the holidays of 2012-13, when Leo arranged my flights and initial hotel booking via Abdou at the Luna Hotel in downtown Cairo.

Let me repeat my original big question: why go to Egypt? Especially to Mother Egypt, as in Mother India or Mother Africa? You go to Egypt as you might return to a source, and in this case to the source of civilization, at least for the Western World. Even if I have not read it anywhere in any of the books on Egypt that I have tried to assimilate—at least I do not recall reading any such statement—it gradually dawned on me that Egypt, more than Mesopotamia or the later Middle East, functioned as the original cradle of civilization for the overall basin of the Mediterranean Sea (really a vast inland ocean between Europe and Africa). Among other contributions Egypt evolved three forms of writing, hieroglyphic, hieratic, and demotic, the last the simplest and the best for everyday use.

The nearby Phoenician traders and merchants adopted this demotic writing and spread it everywhere they went throughout the Mediterranean and beyond, out into the Atlantic Ocean and the nearby islands, including Britain. These other people in turn adopted the demotic-Phoenician alphabet, and it became the basis for the Greek and Latin alphabets, in turn adapted to other languages, such as the Greek for the Cyrillic alphabet used for the Russian language. The ancient world did not perceive or conceive of time in the same linear manner as we do in the modern world, and for the emerging Hellenic and Roman world Egypt appeared as a constant, as an eternal phenomenon. *No one could remember a time when Egypt had not existed*. Thus for us today the remnants of her ancient civilization, her temples and pyramids and obelisks, possess a talismanic or magical quality, symbolizing a still potent sense of continuity, that rarest of states or conditions, given the often chaotic or destructive nature of the human experience on this planet.

Therefore, to visit Egypt for us in the West represents a return to the original matrix that gave birth eventually to our own civilization. Thus it was with this understanding of what Egypt represented and still represents that I went forth to make a deeply experienced, if not indeed a sentimental, pilgrimage to the Land of the Nile during February and March of 2013. The flesh may have seemed weak and frail at times, inasmuch as I did feel on occasion a certain existential anxiety, but the heart beat strong with a true and choice emotion of piety while I made my pilgrimage, rather like the prodigal son, back to the ancient and still enduring household of his parents, in this case back to our home known as Mother Egypt.

My original plan went as follows: leaving on 10 February, four weeks in Egypt, L.A. to London to Cairo; and then, leaving Cairo on 10 March, two weeks in Thailand (staying with a friend in Koh Samui), Cairo to Bangkok to L.A., returning on 24 March. Leo had arranged all my flights for around $2000, and had booked me into the Luna Hotel for a few nights as my initial base. Abdou would meet me at the airport and convey me to my lodging. Per my original plan for Egypt, I would first see the major sites from Cairo in the north all the way to Abu Simbel in the south, the latter some 1400 or 1500 miles from the equator. Then back to Cairo, I would visit St. Catherine's Monastery (in the Sinai Peninsula), Alexandria, and Siwah the great oasis 400 miles or so southwest of Alexandria or Cairo for that matter.

As originally laid out, this plan might seem rather ambitious, but a great and good friend of mine, John Miller, had achieved something similar, and with plenty of time. However, as things turned out, the death of my close friend Rah Hoffman, with whom I have lived for the last fourteen years, intervened (he died on 24 February)—I would have to return and settle his estate—and I came back home on 1 March, Leo rearranging my flights from Cairo to Munich to L.A. Nonetheless, I had experienced by that time all the major sites; and I plan to return to Egypt at some future time (not overly remote) for another three or four weeks, to finish that part of my original itinerary taking place in northern or Lower Egypt, Alexandria, the Sinai, Siwah, etc. Once I had received the news of Rah's death, I could not in good conscience dillydally here and there while the need to settle his estate was hanging over my head like the Sword of Damocles.

A special word on money, with a bit of historic background. Beginning with the "infamous" Lord Cromer (who at least re-established Egypt's finances on a vastly improved basis), the British occupied and controlled Egypt from 1882 until 1952, first and foremost because of the Suez Canal and their need for an unimpeded passage to and from India that the waterway permitted. This "veiled protectorate" endured until 1952, when Colonel Gamal Abdel Nasser heading a group of officers in the Egyptian Army forced both the puppet King Farouk and the British to leave, and the Egyptians established the official Republic of Egypt, their first period of self-rule since the last pharaohs (nominally the Ptolemaic Dynasty). Not surprisingly, modern Egypt has modeled its money, the Egyptian pound, after the British pound. Only the Egyptian pound in no way possesses the current value of the British one. As of the moment, on the black market (courtesy of some of the money exchanges in Cairo), 7 Egyptian pounds equal one U.S. dollar.

As arranged by Leo, I left LAX mid-evening, Sunday, 10 February 2012 via British Airways, stopping off at London's Heathrow Airport for several hours, and then continuing to Cairo, arriving there early in the morning of 12 February, where (as planned) Abdou met me, holding a placard with my name on it, once I got out of customs. We introduced ourselves, and in an hour or so I found myself at the front desk of the Luna Hotel in downtown Cairo, signing my name. Soon after that I had settled in my room, and mercifully fell asleep at once.

Once I woke up mid-morning, somewhat refreshed, I dressed and ate the breakfast that came as usual with the room. It consisted of fruit juice, coffee, and a couple of tasty rolls with butter, but on Abdou's advice I soon switched to the Egyptian breakfast consisting of two bread pockets, one filled with beans, the other with a mixture of fresh vegetables. Abdou made an appearance, and we planned and plotted my itinerary, of which Leo had already sent him a copy by email. The itinerary focussed on three or four chief locales or cities, not only in and of themselves, but also as chief points from which to make collateral trips: Cairo, Louqsor, Aswan, and Alexandria. Thus, traditionally, they have served for many other visitors in Egypt. During that first week in Cairo, while driving me from place to place, Abdou was also arranging the main part of my Nilotic sojourn with his network of collaborators using his magical cell phone.

The safari plan went about as follows. First, around a week in Cairo. There Abdou would act as my driver and practical guide. Second, a week in and around Louqsor (ancient Waset or Thebes), West and East Banks. Third, a week or less between Louqsor and Aswan, including the boat cruise for three days and three nights between Louqsor and Aswan, with a night or so in the latter. In Louqsor I would have several drivers, but Medon would act as my main Egyptological guide at the sites, as well as the overall agent hiring others. In Aswan, Mahmoud would act as the agent for other drivers and Egyptological guides. Fourth, a final week, back to Cairo, and then onward to the Sinai, Alexandria, and Siwah. This would remain as the last week to plan or arrange, which Abdou could arrange before my return to Cairo or almost at the last minute.

Tuesday, 12 February. Escorted there by Abdou, I spent most of my first day in Egypt at the incomparable Egyptian Museum, a big and handsome structure, an easy ten-minute walk from the hotel. It easily contains the best Egyptiana that have managed to survive from ancient times, thus the crème de la crème, but had not most of it lain hidden for millennia these beautiful objects would have long ago disappeared. A sad and sobering fact: the collection in the museum represents only a tiny fraction of the extraordinary beauty that the ancient Egyptians created.

People wonder why I don't take photos, or if I do, but rarely. (I do take notes, however, possibly more personal than photos.) In Egypt's case, so many superb color photos, along with black and white ones, already exist as taken by first-rate and often professional photographers, and as extant in many large coffee-table books (some even seem the size of a small coffee table!), that it seems fruitless to take my own. Let the reader go search these books out wherever they exist (usually in libraries) and feast his vision upon them. Another reason why I don't take photos: to do justice to structures, to architecture, a photographer needs first-rate and expensive equipment, involving many factors like filters, sunlight, moonlight, angle of perspective, etc. Thus you spend valuable time at a given site immersed in taking pictures but not experiencing the site itself, the atmosphere, the charm of the location.

Wednesday, 13 February. I established my preferred pattern for visiting the sites ancient and medieval on my second day in Egypt. Abdou drove me to Saqqara first and then to the Great Pyramids further north, all on the west bank of the Nile. He drives the hotel owner's private vehicle, usually kept when not in use in a parking lot not far from the hotel. After I dawdled and walked around for a while at Djoser's (and Imhotep's) step pyramid and the immediate area (I would return to Saqqara on my last day in Egypt), we drove next to the Great Pyramids, but parked in the village below, at a place where people can hire a horse, a camel, or a horse and carriage, to go to and from the gigantic pyramids, three in number.

To avoid the crush of tourists and hustlers at the main entrance, Abdou had me get out here and hire a calèche and horse as driven in this case by a charming young man Raycup. (I spell these names as I heard them and noted them down.) He came of a Bedouin family that owned and operated a farm in the echt-fertile Fayoum some 50 miles southwest of Cairo. Raycup much enjoys his job as a carriage-driver for the tourists. Under his aegis I visited two of the largest pyramids and then the Sphinx, which you cannot approach too closely, and which sits with its own temples in its own rather large enclosure.

What can I say concerning the Great Pyramids that someone else had not already said? Colossal, overwhelming, mindboggling, breathtaking? They survive as literally man-made mountains. Raycup had me get out of the calèche and get up close to touch the biggest pyramid, the one built by Cheops or Khufu. All three pyramids must have looked stunning when they had their original outer envelope of limestone blocks, and before the Arabs quarried them for buildings in Fustat and Cairo during Early Islam. Inspired by the example of some amiable and fun-loving Egyptian teenagers, I even boosted myself on top of the first row of colossal blocks that make up the bulk of the greatest pyramid. Only their size has prevented them from later people quarrying them in turn, unless (as recently reported) some madman blows them up (if that is possible) because they are survivals from a pagan past—that is, as he and others have threatened to do.

The collective ascendancy of the young Egyptians and myself did not last long: some guards appeared and ordered us off. I got back in the calèche, and next Raycup drove me to the enclosure around the Sphinx, looking purty good considering its age (4000 or 5000 years?), even if necessarily somewhat repaired and restored. Like the pyramids, it creates a unique and extraordinary impression. I looked at it long and hard, but the Sphinx did not bother to return the courtesy. Following this, Raycup drove me back to the village below, where Abdou awaited me not far from his car, and then drove me back to the hotel. Possibly overtipping him, I gave Raycup 100 Egyptian pounds, the most that I tipped anyone in Egypt, that is, apart from Abdou in Cairo, Medon in Louqsor, and Mahmoud in Aswan. I don't regret the gesture: Raycup's dexterous driving, his charm, and his sense of shared fun deserved nothing less!

The night of Wednesday, 13 February, that very night, I had trouble sleeping due to a subtle and persistent noise. I went up to the front desk on the fifth floor and asked for a change of chamber. Omar, the kind and accommodating man on duty, let me switch from Room 307 to Room 312. The new chamber with its blessèd quietude suited me perfectly, and from that time forward I inhabited that room whenever I stayed in the hotel.

Thursday, 14 February. In case I failed to mention it, Cairo spreads out over an enormous area: it must rank as one of the largest cities that I have ever visited, up there with L.A., New York, London, and Bangkok. Driving at a sensible speed, it still takes a while to get in and out of the central or downtown part of Cairo, where the Luna's building stands with five or six stories that include the two floors, three and five, that make up the Luna Hotel. Other businesses occupy the same building, and some families reside here and there on the same floors, an interesting mix.

Just before leaving the hotel that morning, Abdou relayed some bad news to me from Leo over the Internet. Rah fell and broke his left hip in the kitchen. Looking after him as usual in my absence, Steven Reschetar found him and had him ambulanced to the hospital in Marina del Rey, where the surgeons patched him up. Next he would need to go to a convalescent home in Playa del Rey for several months before he could return to his own home. Since Rah was receiving excellent care, and since I could achieve nothing by returning at once to L.A., Leo advised me to continue my travels at least in Egypt. Good advice!

Today Abdou and I leapt forward in time from Ancient Egypt to Early Islam and the Arab settlement in the Middle Ages. We visited the Old City (most of it Islamic), the Coptic Quarter, and the site of El Fustat, the city that preceded Cairo. Not far from the Souk of El Fustat (a modern edifice), the first mosque built in Egypt still endures. Taking off our shoes, Abdou and I entered; we saw no one else, and we both prayed in the Islamic fashion. We then wandered around the Coptic Quarter, visiting several churches and a synagogue-museum.

We had a real epiphany when we went into the very last church, and I consummated one of my most fervent wishes! A priest was conducting a service in Coptic and was chanting in that language, the only usage where the old Egyptian tongue survives. I have heard the language spoken long ago during the long Pharaonic period! The priest chants in Hamitic in a style nearly identical to that of the call to prayer in Arabic. In a certain way this chance encounter with Coptic thrilled me more than visiting the Great Pyramids.

Leaving the Old City, we drove next to the magnificent Citadel between Old Cairo and modern downtown Cairo, still some real distance away. Saladin, or Salah-uh-Din, established the extensive fortress on a very broad and fairly high hill. It includes the National Police Museum (rather small) and the National Military Museum, the latter a real palace on several floors with outstanding displays, models, busts, and other statuary of excellent quality. Both before and after visiting this last museum (which I found fascinating despite myself), I went by and looked in at the gigantic central mosque that dominates the Citadel as the summit of the lofty hill. I also took advantage of the site to look from the battlements out over much of Old Cairo to the west, south, and north—a wonderful panorama, very different in kind from looking out from the top of a skyscraper. Although now early afternoon, it seemed like a very full day, and one deeply satisfying. Abdou drove back to the hotel, and I retired to my chamber for a shower and a rest.

Friday, 15 February. In Egypt Friday and Saturday make up the weekend, with Friday the Muslim Sabbath, a day of rest for many people, and in the case of Abdou, quite well deserved. But he had arranged for me to remain at the hotel until 6:30 P.M., when a driver would take me to the railroad station in Gizeh for the overnight "sleeper" train to Louqsor. Friday thus turned into my first free day. I would walk around central Cairo, revisiting the Egyptian Museum, and just sauntering here and there, but never too far from the hotel. My first visit to the museum, Tuesday, 12 February, lasted from 1:30 to 4:30 in the afternoon. Abdou escorted me there and then back to the hotel, meeting me outside at the exit at the northwest end of the museum.

As we rounded the southwest corner going toward the front, we encountered a very cute and very small beige cat with brown stripes, rather suggesting a jungle cat in miniature. I made that moist puckering sound used to call cats, and it ran right up to me. I now perceived that it was only a kitten, one of the cutest and healthiest that I had seen in a very long time. It must have belonged to some litter nestled somewhere on the museum grounds. As I caressed it gently—lower jaw, head, behind the ears—it reared up to my touch. Carefully I picked it up with one hand, and before it could protest, I kissed it on the head (it smelled sweet and clean), placed it down gently, and watched it run off along the western side of the museum. When I returned on Friday and walked around the structure (encased inside its iron grille-work fence), I looked for the little cat and called to it at the southwest corner, but by happenstance we did not meet again. Still, it left me a very sweet memory.

My driver arrived and met me at the front desk, and then drove me and my two bags to the railroad station in Gizeh with plenty of time for its departure at 8:00 P.M. Alas, all the trains ran late that evening, and we did not leave until 10:15. But at last I found myself in my own private cabin, and moreover just a short distance from the restroom. The obliging young steward brought my dinner at once and made my bed soon after that. For some reason I slept very poorly that night, thus guaranteeing that I would sleep very well at my hotel the next night in Louqsor! However, the breakfast next morning served to restore my energy and my equanimity. The train arrived in Louqsor at 9 A.M. more or less on time.

A young man, Mohammed, drove me to the very good mid-range Gaddis Hotel, where I soon settled in at my new room, taking a short and restorative nap. In the early afternoon I met in the lobby my new chief guide (both practical and Egyptological), "Medon," with whom I would go to all the chief sites in and around Louqsor, both banks of the Nile. I canceled the day, explaining my lack of sleep. Medon understood, and we arranged to meet in the morning for our first outing. I slept much of the afternoon and came down to eat my evening meal in the large and excellent restaurant in the hotel. Since the Gaddis caters to tourists, they can order whatever alcoholic beverage they might want, in spite of the Muslim ban against liquor. The hotel maintains a full bar, amusingly decorated with Hathor columns (among other jocular motifs), whose capitals carry, instead of Hathor's face and head, the bearded faces of modern tourists wearing sunglasses. These and other parodistic motifs always made me chuckle and put me in a good humor while I sat there, drinking a beer or a luscious cocktail.

With a good meal and a good beverage thus ended the first of my six days based in Louqsor, from Saturday, 16 February, through Thursday, 21 February. I went to bed early, and in fact slept very well despite the first call to prayer at 5 A.M. from the big nearby mosque (just north of the hotel) that had the loudest of loudspeakers on its neon-lit minaret. I soon learned by heart that the calls to prayer took place at 5:00 A.M., 12 noon, 3:30, 5:30, and 7:00 P.M.; and I also soon learned to sleep in between those appointed hours. I had not noticed any calls to prayer while in Cairo, at least not in the downtown.

Sunday, 17 February. Next morning I woke up much refreshed and ready for the two chief sites on the East Bank, the temples at Karnak and Louqsor proper, the latter not more than a mile or so north or northeast of the Gaddis Hotel. The Corniche, the major waterside avenue or boulevard—always called thus, whether by the Nile or fronting on the Mediterranean (as in the case of Alexandria and other cities on the northern seacoast)—lay just five minutes or so to the west. Being a hotel of some scope, the Gaddis offers quite a good buffet for breakfast (but located in a smaller restaurant a floor above to one side of the outdoor pool): a variety of meats and vegetables, different types of rolls, hot beverages, fruit juice, etc., all very tasty and not over-spicy, the latter usually not agreeing with me. The hotel guest also may order an omelette or some other egg dish.

We got going early, as usual around 8 A.M., sometimes a half hour later. Medon with driver showed up on time, as they generally did. The temple complex at Karnak, especially the Temple of Amun, I can only call gigantic, the latter as the biggest religious edifice on the planet, even larger than the Vatican's papal basilica or Angkor Wat in Cambodia, even if both of those remain quite impressive in their own way. Covering some 5500 square meters and boasting a forest of 134 gigantic papyrus-inspired columns (the four ones in the central aisle are nothing less than humongous), the Great Hypostyle Hall inspires a wonder and awe nearly akin to fear. Several gigantic cathedrals could easily fit onto this acreage. Even Medon as a professional, college-trained guide remains impressed by this hall after all his years of experience and after many tourists. He is a young adult. His expert commentary communicates both information and enthusiasm. Medon is not merely an excellent (practical and Egyptological) guide—he really knows his material—but is also a very pleasant companion with a great sense of humor, always a nice combination under any circumstances.

While on a smaller scale, the Louqsor temple is quite impressive and even exquisite in its own way. It survives more intact than the chief temple at Karnak. To the north of the Louqsor site the avenue of ram-headed sphinxes once ran complete all the way to the avenue's beginning at the Temple of Amun 3 kilometers just north of the Louqsor temple. That particular section measures as the longest and the most intact. You must recreate in your imagination how these fanes must have appeared in their prime: brilliantly painted, with banners flapping on their flagstaffs ensconced on the front of their pylons; flashing with gold, silver, copper, and electrum; alive with people and statues of all types (the latter both large and small); priests and officials coming and going, along with people furnishing provisions for use by the temple personnel. After you pass the ticket booth to the west of the Temple of Amun, you will find something that will help you visualize the fane in all its splendor and size: a very large-scale model of the entire temple complex that imparts an excellent concept of what it once looked like on its 62 acres.

Some years agone I had read about the Louqsor temple in a special book, an archaeological report, extant in UCLA's Research Library. In the third century C.E. the Romans had changed the temple into a fortress, augmenting the total walled area by about a half, expanding to the west and especially to the southeast, However, the Roman remains lie buried or (rather) re-buried. You can easily perceive how readily the Romans could have changed the temple into a fortress, given the wall-enclosed structure of the original building.

(This first outing with Medon during Sunday, 17 February, had turned into a particularly rewarding day and augured well for the rest of my sojourn in Louqsor.)

Monday, 18 February. This marks my first visit to the West Bank, a region of tombs and funerary temples that survive in varying degrees of intactness. On the agenda today we shall go to the Valley of the Kings, the Maat Factory in the village of El-Korna, Deir Al-Bahari, and the Colossi of Memnon. Incidentally, the professional guides need not pay to enter the official sites, nor does the tourist need to pay for the guide to enter. The visitor will still need to tip both driver and guide at the end of the given outing. Because I had read extensively before going to Egypt, I already knew much about most of the sites that I wanted to visit. Nevertheless, the guide's own presentation served to refresh my memory or to focus on some new detail or nuance impossible to learn in advance.

After passing through the entrance building along with Medon and purchasing my ticket, we got into one of the covered (metal) wagons pulled by a small uncovered motor vehicle. This motor train takes the tourists to the main area where the tombs begin, some distance away. The highest mountain summit, shaped rather like a pyramid, marks the overall site of the Valley of the Kings (KV), utterly desolate and barren. Tourists can purchase tickets to only three tombs at a time. Since at least 62 tombs exist (not all of them open to the public), it would require quite a bit of time and money to visit them all. Given the general similarity among all these tombs—longer or larger per the given pharaoh's life and reign—the average tourist might choose to visit only a few.

Medon guided me to the first three tombs nearest to the main area of arrival for the motor train. Thus I visited one short (KV2: Ramesses IV), one medium-length (KV6: R. IX), and one quite extended (KV8: Merenptah, who succeeded his father, the great R. II); and these three completely satisfied my own sepulchral interest. The first one, if I recall correctly, seems to have the largest possible limestone sarcophagus (immensely tall). It helped me grasp why such stone coffins manage to survive in place, given their size and weight. For 100 Egyptian pounds you can visit King Tut's tomb; I chose not to do so; the authorities had closed it for a while before my tour in Egypt, and in any event, small and cramped, it lacks the beautiful decorations of the major tombs.

Just before I would fly from Cairo back to L.A., I would visit the celebrated Serapeum at Saqqarra. Even before going there, I suspected (rightly as it turned out) that it would intrigue and fascinate me far more than the tombs in the Valley of the Kings. Before departing from KV, I went up to the locked (outer) metal door to KV5, the so-called Lost Tomb, where Ramesses II buried before his own death many of his highest ranking sons.

While driving from KV en route to the Temple of Hatshepsut at Deir Al-Bahari, we stopped at the Maat Factory in the village of El-Korna, where several cousins own and run a workshop and showroom, in which local artisans make a variety of excellent Egyptological mementos from genuine Egyptian minerals and stones, far superior to the usual souvenirs on sale at many ancient sites. This halt came as a complete surprise but it turned out fine, an overall agreeable interlude. I had wanted to buy some superior mementos for a few special friends, and this halt provided the perfect occasion. One cousin Shahkur was absent, but the two remaining, Ahmed and Hamou, acted as my gracious hosts, Ahmed in his galabiyeh (one-piece gownlike garment worn by many Egyptian men), and Hamou, positively dashing in full Arab regalia including the kaffiyeh on his head. His trim pointed beard and neat moustache only added to his exotic charm, like a character stepping out of some popular novel of the first third of the twentieth century.

Both cousins appeared to speak very good English, but with Medon sitting quietly to one side, Ahmed it was who hosted me in the showroom, pointing out and handing to me the many superior products hand-carved out of crystal, onyx (which has many colors besides black), limestone, basalt, some unusual light green and light blue stone, etc., all suggesting something gemlike. Meanwhile Ahmed treated me to a real Turkish coffee (black, thick, heavily sugared), while Medon and he imbibed some minted tea. Nobody pressured me to buy, but soon I chose a hand-sized scarab carved out of basalt with hieroglyphs on the bottom. While expensive, I happily bought it. Then, grateful for the purchase, Ahmed gave me as a gift a small sculpted cat representing Bastet, the cat goddess, made out of some pretty light blue stone. This would serve as a gift for some other friends or friend. Hamou, incidentally, speaks six languages, and we spoke a little French.

This encounter showed me an aspect of Middle Eastern life that I had read about but did not know still existed, a lesson in gracious business-dealing. Thus fortified by our beverages, Medon and I said farewell and continued on our way to Deir Al-Bahari. Between them Ahmed and Hamon had created an enchanted hour for me, one that I shall always cherish. Should I ever visit Louqsor again, I plan to return to Maat Factory.

Deir Al-Bahari. This especial site, more than Karnak or the Great Pyramids, became an aesthetic experience of the highest order, if not indeed an echt-religious one as well for the same reason. In 1947 (after World War II had finally come to an end) my mother Annette, my uncle Roland (her brother), my brother Ronald, and I visited some close relatives in Brooklyn, our first visit to N.Y.C. (apart from Uncle Roland long familiar with the Big Apple). Among other highlights in Manhattan we visited the Metropolitan Museum of Art, which has a scale model of Hatshepsut's memorial temple with the western cliffs immediately above it, as perfect an example of architecture suited to its environment as anything designed by any modern architect. The site creates an oddly modern impression, the lines of the edifice remain so clean and subtly dazzling. The scale model, seen sixty-six years before, came back like a ghost to reinforce my visit to the site in person.

Archaeologists have worked on excavating and restoring this fane since 1891. As already noticed—but it needs emphasis—the location and the temple complement each other to perfection and make an unforgettable ensemble. No modern architect could surpass this complex, designed by Senenmut, architect to Hatshepsut, and (some speculate) possibly her lover. The cliffs lifting up at once at the back of the edifice rise about 1000 feet in a very dramatic way. At the foot of the first ramp going up into the higher temple—among other items revealed by excavation—you should not miss the roots (yes, the roots) of some exotic incense-bearing trees or bushes brought back from the queen's famous expedition to Punt. How strangely poignant that we can still observe the roots of those little trees planted or transplanted over three thousand years before!

If ever I return to Louqsor, I must go back not only to the Maat Factory but more particularly to Deir Al-Bahari, not to mention the final site that we visited on that outing before we went back to the Gaddis Hotel: the Colossi of Memnon (no fee needed to be paid here—how rare!), which with their original double crowns must have measured as two of the largest such statues ever made (at least 60 feet high) and put into place. Thus ended another very full and satisfying excursion!

An aside. Because I'm publishing this report privately and sending it only to close friends, I shall add some information about my two chief guides that I might not include in an article intended for a nationally distributed magazine—information that is personal but not intimate. I can certainly recommend both Abdou and Medon in their professional status as practical and/or Egyptological guides. More than that, I can recommend them, and with pleasure, in a moral or ethical sense as kind as well as benevolent and beneficent individuals.

For example, in the case of Abdou, I directly witnessed several acts of unusual kindness toward both beast and man. Whenever he drives out to certain sites, e.g., Saqqara, while ciceroning tourists like myself, he generally brings along with him food that he has prepared to distribute to the stray dogs that hang out there, not something that many natives might think to do in Egypt, where many people seem to be homeless in the big cities and to go hungry. For another example, in the late afternoon close to the Egyptian Museum, Abdou helped a flustered young man, a backpacker from Paris, to ascertain (by Abdou's portable telephone) the correct time (at 6:00 P.M.) and location for a bus leaving Cairo for Farafra's town and oasis (about 300 miles to the southwest of Cairo), and then hailing a taxi for him so he could get to the correct bus station in time to buy his ticket and get safely on board. Apart from those examples, I need only mention the numerous kindnesses that Abdou did for myself as a sometimes anxious tourist, and for whom he prepared an itinerary (Cairo to Louqsor to Aswan and then back to Cairo) that proceeded with the utmost smoothness, comfort, and courtesy.

As for the genial and responsible Medon, he excels at his profession, which he loves. Medon is married, is a licensed tour guide, has a university degree, and a daughter one year old, Asil (pronounced ah-SEEL). Families here in Egypt are in general very close. Medon and his own family live on the first floor of his house (their house, that of husband and wife). He has his father and mother, whom he dearly loves, living on the floor above his family. He also has his brother living with him on the same floor. They all eat their meals together. His wife does not work outside the home but takes care of the home, the family, the management of the domestic scene, including the making of the meals. Many American families could not improve on this and might well envy Medon's domestic arrangement.

Tuesday, 19 February. Today a new driver, Sayed, took Medon and myself to the two funerary temples not far from Hatshepsut's at Deir Al-Bahari: first, the Ramesseum (of R. II) is a relatively small temple somewhat like that at Louqsor (i.e., as compared to Karnak or Abu Simbel), and like that at Louqsor also rather exquisite. In addition, it represents an impressive and ongoing job of reconstruction since the latter nineteenth century, like the site at Deir Al-Bahari. Odd, but I found an abalone shell beyond the temple's rear among the sun-dried brick walls (old and evidently reconstructed): how the shell got there, I have no idea, but its unexpected iridescence imparted a maritime charm to the locale.

Both temples face or open on the southeast. You enter the Ramesseum from the right side (facing the front) but not through the original pylon, incompletely restored. Near the second pylon sit the remains of a colossal statue of R. II, larger even than the Colossi of Memnon (actually Amenhotep III, at least as great a ruler as R. II), much of it still all in one piece. To reconstruct the statue alone would require a giant industrial crane like those used in massive (modern) construction projects. The statue fell and shattered in an especially violent earthquake. The head and upper torso survive more or less intact, still rather remarkable considering how much time has passed since the very long life and reign of R. II during the 1200s B.C.E.

Medinat Habu, built for and by Ramesses III, extends about 1000 feet from front to rear and survives as one of the best-preserved temples—that is, apart from some of the columns, of which only the bases and lower parts exist (the said columns as extant in the hypostyle hall and beyond toward the rear). Instead of the usual-style pylon (two trapezoidal towers joined by a gate in the middle, the standard model), this temple has one modeled after a Syrian-style gatehouse. Even without the parts that are missing (used by Mohammed Ali Pasha to build a nearby sugar factory), this temple of R. III stands as a particularly beautiful and impressive example of an Ancient Egyptian fane.

Another aside. The regular tap water (treated, of course) comes from the Nile. The natives warn the visitors not to drink it (although they can use it for showers, etc.), the latter making do with bottled water. The natives can usually drink the tap water with no ill effect. If tourists drink it, they run the risk of diarrhea or worse. So if the same problem in Mexico constitutes Montezuma's Revenge, then does the tourist diarrhea in Egypt represent Tutankhamun's Curse, King Tut's Revenge, or a Case of the Dire Rear?

Wednesday, 20 February. We have finished with our easy and leisurely tour of the West Bank, at least for the nonce. Today we drive to Dendara (accent on the first syllable), to visit the Hathor Temple there, finished by the Ptolemaic Dynasty, the last native or near-native dynasty to rule Egypt (before Rome took over under Octavian, or Caesar Augustus). The Ptolemies built the inner temple and put the finishing touches on the outer or main temple, one of the few where you can climb (if allowed) up onto the intact stone roof. I had hoped to visit both Abydos and Amarna, but they can wait until some future sojourn in Egypt after the present one. It takes an hour to drive to Dendara from Louqsor, and an hour to drive back, spending perhaps 2 hours at the site. To get to Abydos (well worth it from descriptions), it takes 2½ hours, ditto to return to Louqsor. Amarna would require even longer, and given the amount of time, it would make a better plan to overnight in the small city of Minya and to drive from there to Amarna (lying some 50 miles or more southeast of Minya), again during some future sojourn in Egypt.

How refreshing to travel without much traffic—a real change—for some real distance in a private car! How crowded and chaotic the city streets in Egypt appear, always clogged in the daytime with motor vehicles of all kinds! I shall never again complain about traffic in the U.S. or in L.A.! The trip to Dendara seemed to take forever, but it only took an hour as predicted. The return trip seemed to go somewhat faster. We had yet another new driver, another Abdou, yet also excellent. As we zipped along the country roads (well maintained), often skirting verdant agricultural fields, small but sturdy donkeys would patiently plod along the roadway margins, pulling small wooden wagons, driven by farmers wearing traditional and practical garb.

The temple at Dendara, apparently quite intact, allows the visitor to imagine how all the great fanes throughout the land once looked in their prime, apart from the colors that have faded. The screened-in hypostyle hall with its immense Hathor-headed capitals is indeed enormously impressive. Instead of the usual pylon, you enter the enclosure (the temple faces north) by means of a Syrian-fort-style gate. Tourists may ascend to the roof (most of it accessible) using the western staircase (the square corkscrew stairs), and then descend by the eastern staircase (the easy one-ramp stairs). While on the roof, I inspected the small rooftop rooms, one of which contains the famous Dendara Zodiac, i.e., its plaster facsimile: the original is now housed in the Louvre in Paris. Overall the original temple colors appear not so faded as at other fanes because the roof has protected them from the fierce African sunlight.

Between the gate and the northwest corner of the main temple's courtyard stand two smaller temples called Mammisi with a Coptic basilica between them in turn. The exceptionally beautiful small Temple of Isis, also quite intact, stands just south of the main temple. I walked around the latter twice, once before entering and then after leaving the interior. Since it so seldom rains in Egypt, I was and am both fascinated and intrigued by the gigantic lion-headed rainspouts (loftily positioned on the exterior walls). Why did anyone add those?

Nevertheless, the day—or, rather, that day's outing—had not yet finished. Medon certainly made sure that I received full value for my investment of time and money! After returning to Louqsor but before going back to the Gaddis Hotel, we visited the extraordinary modern Louqsor Museum. In particular the older main part of the edifice has incomparable statues mostly of 18th-Dynasty kings and other eminent people, most of the statues intact, mirabile dictu! One of the most unusual, in gleaming white alabaster, represents the great crocodile god Sobek, protecting the smaller figure of a youthful Amenhotep III. Sobek is dressed as an Egyptian of the 18th Dynasty, and this makes the two figures wonderfully bizarre and unforgettable!

Medon had thoughtfully scheduled the day following, Thursday, as my free day, when I could roam at will around Louqsor on my own, or at least as freely as the many hustlers, taxi and carriage drivers, eager for tourist business, would allow me. I tipped the new driver and Medon rather more generously than the standard tipping suggested; and in the case of Medon, an overall bigger extra tip for the overall four or five days during which, as I warmly acknowledged to him, he had made my itinerary proceed so well, so smoothly, not to mention abundantly. After my free day, a special treat on Friday awaited me, and toward this I looked forward with the greatest anticipation.

Thursday, 21 February. By the time I reach Abu Simbel, I shall probably end up completely templed out, just as I became after visiting all those fanes in Southeast Asia, including Bangkok, Ayutthayuh, and Angkor. For once, because of my free day, I did not need to rush my breakfast to be on time for Medon with driver to pick me up in the hotel's luxurious lobby at 8:00 A.M. I could luxuriantly dawdle before I set out on foot, and then I finally began hiking in various directions into the immediate vicinage radiating from the hotel, but never straying too far. Since this represented my first real chance to walk fast and unhindered since the previous Friday, I was walking with notable speed (even for me, who can outwalk most people); and soon I headed north along the avenue going north from the hotel.

After about 15 minutes I turned into a street going west to the Corniche along the Nile, and continued until I came abreast of the Louqsor Temple set amid its rather large enclosure (along with other buildings), which I circumnavigated west to north to east to south before heading back to the hotel. However, I had no need to rush and often stopped to talk with old and young, absorbing the ambiance. North of the open space before the first pylon there extends a superb avenue of sphinxes, which I had hardly noticed when I first came to the temple with Medon. This avenue had once connected to its début before the huge temple at Karnak, but much later construction lies over most of the main part between the two points. The section just north of the southern temple must measure several hundred feet. Many of these particular sphinxes, but not most of them, survive intact. They must have made a grand appearance in their prime.

By the time that I came back to the hotel, I had enjoyed as brisk a walk as I had so far had in Egypt. No mean feat, when you consider the hustlers, touts, and con men who importune the tourist at almost every turn. Once I returned to the hotel, I spent the rest of the day resting and reading. Overall a pleasant and lazy day, including some good news about Rah in the convalescent hospital or home, where his condition had become stable, and where he was making a steady recovery. Good news, and I could rest easy on that score.

Friday, 22 February. The special treat: the cruise on the Nile from Louqsor to Aswan for three days and three nights now begins! (Chronologically the time on the river covered Friday, 22 February, through Sunday, 24 February.) This cruise turned into the highest point of the entire trip in Egypt, something that I had not expected at all. I had wanted originally to take the cruise on a dahabiyya, but that would have cost me more than what I had budgeted. Abdou in Cairo had wisely shifted me to a regular cruise boat; and as it developed, this became the better choice, simply because a cruise boat has more levels and much more space.

The extraordinary natural beauty of the Nile between Louqsor and Aswan makes the cruise nothing less than idyllic. The rocky hills and cliffs that lift up at some distance to east and west at times come closer to "Egypt's lone monarchal stream" (Ashton Smith, "Memnon at Midnight"), and then at other times appear to draw back dramatically. Between the desert land on either side there flourishes a fairly wide margin right above the river heavily verdant with palm trees of every description—not only date palms with their "beards," that are allowed to grow and to provide shelter for "the little creatures," but also, mixed in with other kinds of trees, other species of palms growing at every height with their circular tops opening out like gigantic fantastical flowers. Breathtaking! This arboreal beauty would bring me on occasion to the verge of tears. Descriptions that I had read in books, or that I had imbibed from the lips of friends who had gone on the same cruise—not to mention from black-and-white as well as full-color photos—had keyed my anticipation to the highest level! I suffered no disappointment in any way.

The actual transit between the two modern cities would only take two days and two nights, docking each night on the Nile's eastern bank (presumably), so that the throbbing of the ship's engines would not disturb the passengers' easy slumber. Sometime around midmorning a driver moved me from the hotel on land to the hotel on water. By late morning I found myself and my two bags (large overnight and small shoulder) ensconced in my stateroom (No. 319), which had a much nicer and more spacious bathroom than at my chamber (No. 307) in the Gaddis Hotel. In fact, my new quarters made up the fanciest accommodations that I enjoyed during my entire Egypt safari. Although I hain't a sybarite or a fancy person about where I sleep or stay (so long as it is quiet for sleeping, napping, etc.), these new quarters proved a most welcome delight, yesh! An emphatic "Melikes it!"

This cruise boat, the *Nile Ruby* (another *Nile Ruby,* No. II, plies the same river), remains fairly typical of all such ships, true floating palaces like the old paddlewheels on the Mississippi. The Nile has no great depth (30 feet?), and consequently the cruise boats do not go deep into the water. The *Nile Ruby* has four stories or five levels: a "basement" floor half in the water with the main dining room; the main floor with lobby and front desk (centrally located, a kind of great hall that extends upwards for another level); the floor above that (my floor, the third one); the fourth floor (with a bar and big TV screen across the room from the bar); finally a top deck with lounge chairs for sunning, reading, or whatever. A small swimming pool nestles at the prow (diveable if you dive shallow and with care). All levels have staterooms.

The top deck divides roughly into thirds: the first third open to the elements; the second or middle third, covered with an awning for those desiring the shade; the last third (at the stern), again open to the elements. The canopied middle has a kind of bar or squarish counter, whence a waiter will dispense tea and cake (a lovely British touch) in the late afternoon: yum! Real wood throughout the ship, and used for the furniture (apart from those ubiquitous plastic chairs on the top deck); and the service people are constantly polishing the brass rails and other fixtures. Not enormous but spacious, the *Nile Ruby* is a typical cruise boat, but some can have more than five levels. They are all constructed with a high central lobby, and they can line up next to one another when docked lengthwise against the quay, so that the passengers from the other (outer) ships can pass through to reach the cement embankment, an arrangement ingenious and eminently practical. Bravo!

No tipping is required aboard ship until the cruise ends (in our case, after the third and last day and night, E£60), but you can tip extra whenever you so desire. Tipping at the bar upstairs is customary. Drinks at the bar or ordered with the meal in the dining room cost extra. The prices for drinks appear quite reasonable: cocktails run about $3.00, and beers about $4.00 (E£20 and E£30, respectively): the prices remind me of those for drinks during the 1940s in the U.S., which decade now seems like a long time agone, when you could have a full-course meal for a dollar or less! Oi vey, Maria!

(Oh, I forgot to add: the staterooms have heavy lined floor-length drapes that open and close at the middle: between them and the glass of the large big-view window [actually divided into two glass panels with a thin divider between them] hangs a thin gauzelike curtain. The drapes block out both light and some sound when the boat docks at some embankment.)

Once the boat got underway, the powerful, oil-fueled engines throbbing (you felt it throughout the ship), all on board were launched into another and marvelous dimension. I sighed a great big sigh! As if the flight (literally, the fleeing) from L.A. and the escape into a thaumaturgical compound of Ancient and Modern Egypt had not sufficed, once more I was escaping along with other refugees (some of them from the bitter cold of Northern Europe) yet further, deeper, into a dreamlike existence (relatively free from any temporal angst about room and board) that would endure for an enchanted period of time and space!

Necessity had dictated that I eat a hurried breakfast, but soon I descended from my chamber to the dining room to have a small but leisurely lunch—excellent food, excellently served buffet-style—with which I drank a beer (Stella, from Alsace-Lorraine, I believe)—a good blond beer, but one that I like less than the Saqqara (a tasty Egyptian brew) that I drank with some of my meals while at the Gaddis Hotel. I had noted how fast the boat was going, once under way. After lunch I went up to the top deck, and agreeably warm, I sat in the midsection under the awning. I might have slept better the night before; but now the amalgam of sudden fatigue, adequate food, the release from tension, and the lack of sleep had made me unduly sensitive.

The beauty of the landscape and the riverscape brought me close to tears. The recollection of Rah's recent fall and convalescence (a mixture of sadness and compassion) added to my mix of emotions as well. Well, I reflected, I had finally made the long-planned entrance into Egypt, and here I sat ensconced on the top deck of a cruise boat. What more could I want? For the first time, while traveling up the Nile southward against the current, I felt a genuine sense of magic and release, a feeling such as I had not felt in quite some little time. Thank you, dear Goddess! And might she not be Isis herself? After duly communing with my immediate ambiance, I descended to my room and took a long and refreshing nap despite the throbbing of the ship's engines.

A nice touch! (Nice? Yes, at once precise and agreeable!) The individual room key attaches to a heavy brass piece, copper-colored, probably 2 by 4 inches, charmingly shaped like an ancient Egyptian cartouche (a long rectangle with rounded corners). Copper, brass (copper and zinc), and bronze (copper and tin), the latter alloys coming into existence to make the copper stronger, all of them eventually overtaken by iron for weaponry. Because Egypt failed to keep up with the metallurgical advance, not because of any lack in her stalwart soldiers, she fell to various invaders—the Hyksos, the Libyans, the Assyrians, the Persians, and lastly the Greeks and the Romans, even if the Greeks under Alexandros Megalos, or Alexander Magnus, received an ecstatic welcome from the Egyptians for their deliverance from the Persians, whom they did not like at all, an understatement.

We shall pass Esna during the night, a temple that I had hoped to visit; perhaps I can do this during a future Egypt safari. Esna has prime importance because of its rare status as an intact structure (including the roof!), but of which only the hypostyle hall has received a full revelation or uncovering. The sun sets in a gray haze. The eastern bank here has palms of every type and size all along the river's edge, outlined against the dark beige mountain ranges of the eastern desert. Incredibly picturesque: lush, lavish greenery! Yum, yum, eat it up! The Nile valley here extends rather far to the eastern and western (low) mountain ranges, 30 miles or more between them, a datum vouchsafed by Amero, a charming young man who dispensed us tea and cake at 4:30 P.M. on the top deck at that counter toward the stern. The deck has three flights of stairs reaching up to it, clearly visible, at the prow, in the middle, and at the stern.

(Re-reading the entry for Friday, 22 February, I can see that I have devoted more space to it than to any other day to date. For that reason I shall try to write more succinctly concerning the remaining days on my itinerary [and the consequent number of total pages], so as to keep down the cost of the photocopies that I intend to give certain close friends. So be it!)

Saturday, 23 February. Sometime early on in the night the ship docked at the quay for Edfu, and the engines fell silent. After a decent night's rest I woke up refreshed, and after an early breakfast I waited on the 8:00 call for the ride to the Edfu Temple, after taking a seat in the lobby. The breakfast, like the lunch and supper of the day before, turned out excellent and was served with similar professionalism. I'm not a "foodie," but I shan't miss a single one of these meals; besides, I'm paying for them! When traveling, I usually restrict myself to morning and evening meals.

The 8:00 call came, and ascending the stairs from the quay to the street above, those of us who have elected to go found a squad of horses and carriages awaiting us. In no time at all we were rolling merrily along to the temple, a 15-minute ride each way there and back. Our carriage held four of us: an Egyptian matron and the cute young Hindi couple who eat at the same table as I do in the dining room, both of them engineers on vacation from Mumbai, both speaking flawless English. We all helped the matron in and out of the carriage; somewhat heavy and swathed in black Muslim-style dress and scarf, she could not walk very fast and kept falling behind. I had to keep reminding the guide, another Mohammed, to wait up for her.

The temple itself proved as much of a treat as the one at Dendara, and as complete, with roof intact, and with the same type of stairs, corkscrew on one side and one long ramp on the other. But here the policy does not permit the visitors to ascend to the roof, no reason given. Whereas Dendara faces north, Edfu faces south. Faint vestiges of color still exist on the walls, in particular when protected from the strong African sunlight. We really did not need such a detailed presentation as we got from the guide—at least I did not—but I still tipped him the usual E£10, of course. What might Egypt have looked like when she still had hundreds of complete fanes like this one?

As ever, I find a certain poignancy in the survival of temples like Dendara and Edfu. How long these places have accidentally lasted and outlasted the people who built them, who worked in them, and who maintained them! Did they ever ponder what would happen to them in the future, and how many invasions their Egypt would endure before exotic outlanders would come purely to visit their structures, and awestruck would marvel at them? Or did those long-ago natives think that the Egypt that they knew might last forever? Who knows?

Meanwhile Modern Egypt has its own unexpected marvels. In the West women usually clean and maintain hotel rooms and so forth, but in Egypt men usually perform this function. A small crew of male workers does the same on the cruise boats. The individual who handled my stateroom, a gentle and witty man, had prepared a delectable surprise for me. When I returned to my chamber in the late morning, what should I discover there waiting for me? On one of the twin beds sat quite an inventive soft sculpture, an elephant, made up out of the towels from the bathroom, complete with tusks, and with two small green pieces of adhesive paper for the eyes! When I saw this, I broke into delighted laughter. Nice, neat, nifty! What fun! I sought the man out at once, thanked him for his ingenious art (conceding it as an utter surprise), and gave him a E£5 note, very well deserved. Later, when talking with some fellow tourists on the top deck, I found out that the same worker also makes crocodiles out of the bathroom towels. The one that he made for them had a box of Kleenex placed as prey between its jaws. I hated breaking my sculpture down, but I did need to use the towels!

Since I had not had a chance to swim in any outdoor pool near home since last November, I eagerly anticipated swimming in the one on the top deck. I tested the water with my hand. Cool but not cold, and basically comfortable. Donning my black Speedo trunks, I took a couple of dips in the shallow water, swimming dogstyle, and even managing to swim underwater several times. Quite an exotic adventure to swim in the prow while the boat plowed relentlessly through the Nilotic waters, passing islands big and small (some with trees, some with cattle grazing), not to mention the ever palm-fringed shores, ever verdant. I prefer by far the cruise boat to a dahabiyya (even if I'm willing to try the latter out on a future occasion), not just because of the cost-saving but because of the multiple decks and the greater spaciousness. Before swimming, I did my usual half-hour of exercises in my stateroom. Between the two activities I felt invigorated. After drying out in the warm sunlight on a recliner chair, I prepared for lunch, which turned into a sumptuous affair: it would have made a sizeable dinner! Perfectly relaxed, I took a nap in my stateroom, and this prepared me for the second and final outing for that same day.

Kom Ombo! The place that the Greeks called Ombos. After docking, we ascended and walked to the temple with ease and in only a few minutes. The same basic type of temple as at Dendara or Edfu, only here the fane, facing southwest, stands in ruins, magnificent and evocative, but still in ruins. Somewhat oddly, the temple divides itself down the middle with columns and other elements, and is located on a dramatic promontory, below which in the ancient period the sacred crocodiles would sun themselves on the river bank. The original pylon is largely eroded and gone. On the left the temple is dedicated to Haroeris, or Horus the Elder; on the right, to Sobek, the crocodile god. Some little distance to the north stands a kind of museum annex with a display of crocodiles (i.e., representations), Sobek, etc.

In its prime this temple must have counted as a special and uniquely beautiful fane, basically a Ptolemaic structure. Many traces of the original colors exist in reasonably vivid state, blue, red, etc., rather a remarkable thing considering that they are over 2000 years old! We visited here between 4:15 and 5:15 P.M., thus in the late afternoon. Just as we were heading back to the ship, I saw (of all people) Medon not far to the north, escorting some tourists, a couple. We recognized each other, I ran up to him, we embraced, said a few words to each other, and then I returned to the ship pronto. What a rush to see him again so unexpectedly! A big buffet dinner, excellent as usual, capped a long and very full day. I had a cocktail with dinner; I ate well but not excessively. Sometime tonight we dock at Aswan.

Sunday, 24 February. Once we got under way following Kom Ombo, the boat made very good time. By 10:00 P.M. we had arrived in Aswan at the quay. Facing west from high on the east bank, it looks like a completely modern city from where we have come to rest. I noted no mosques nearby, and I prayed that I would be spared the call to prayer by those extra-loud loudspeakers like those near the Gaddis Hotel in Louqsor. (Amen!) Some kind fate granted me my wish (I write eight hours later). No call to prayer shattered my slumber. Once again I managed to get a good night's rest and woke up quite refreshed. Jubilation!

At breakfast I missed the charming Hindi couple, who got up much earlier, ate a hurried breakfast, and left at 3:30 A.M. to take the bus (the minivans) to Abu Simbel and back. But I shall see them again later on. They have the happy mood that young adults usually have while on vacation. Altogether, a delightful and physically beautiful couple! They have made our meals at the same table quite an enjoyable experience. They speak at least three languages: Hindi, the Hindi-related lingo of the state where they reside (Mumbai), and English. By comparison, how language-deprived the average American seems, speaking only one language and knowing literature in only that one tongue!

Mahmoud, the agent in Aswan employed by Abdou in Cairo, met me for the first time in the lobby between 9:00 and 9:30 A.M. to discuss and lay out the schedule for my sojourn while based in this town. I shall eat a light and early lunch so as to be ready for departure at 2:00 P.M. for the big outing to the High Dam and Philae-Agilkia. Until then I have four free hours to use as I wish. Thus liberated, I meandered my way to the ATM in the bank across the street from the boat to get more small cash for today's adventures and later. Possibly a mistake, I walked along the eastern or inland side of Aswan's Corniche (not so simple due to the shops, hustlers, and shopkeepers) all the way to my goal on the same street going south, the new and resplendent Coptic Cathedral, a huge landmark involving a real compound and an impressive Bishop's Palace (or so it seemed to me), the latter not quite finished. A very gracious lady (a volunteer worker) assured me that, of course, I could sit and commune in the cathedral, which I did.

I shall describe my impressions of this temple, but later: overall, an inspiring experience. Egyptian Christianity, part of the Eastern Church, not only figures as the earliest in Christendom, but includes the original founder of the first monastery (in Egypt's Eastern Desert), the St. Anthony celebrated in literature, especially *La Tentation de Saint-Antoine,* by Gustave Flaubert, an uniquely superb and extended *poème en prose,* which also exists in Lafcadio Hearn's equivalently magnificent English translation (a masterpiece). Flaubert, not at all incidentally, did in fact voyage in Egypt with his friend Maxime du Camp and wrote a record of it. I could not linger in the cathedral unduly, but as I left to return to the cruise boat along the western or outer side of the Corniche (no human obstacles!), I noted for another time, across the street from the cathedral, a very large enclosure (inside an iron-rod fence), the Ferial Gardens, a lovely verdant oasis-park (E£5 to enter, open from 8:00 A.M. to 8:00 P.M.), where people may picnic and have other family outings, but the place has its own coffee shop. A striking, very dark man in galabiyeh and Arab head-cover, the soul of affability, sat in the ticket office at the entrance, dispensing both tickets and information. He spoke excellent English in a deep melodious voice.

Some quick impressions of the Coptic Cathedral in Aswan, the second largest in Egypt and North Africa (that is, after Cairo). Despite myself, with no expectations, my visit inside this temple turned into a very moving (religious) experience. (Wow! Hallelujah! Gloria in excelsis Deo!) The Coptic Church in general does not use the regular church organ during services, but only singing. In addition, the priest chants the liturgy in Coptic, a sound as astonishing and unforgettable as (and similar to) the Arab call to prayer (we speak here in both cases of an art that must be learned and mastered).

The cathedral itself is enormous and can comfortably contain somewhere between 3000 and 5000 people. The pews are all made out of imported American oak (a huge expense). The interior is painted in a light yellow color; and the window glass in the large tall windows has almost the same color, translucent but not transparent.

All this combines in such a way that the temple glows inside with light, and with a feeling of lightness (imponderability). A few small round stained-glass windows are positioned way up high on the walls, but do not in any way mitigate the overall effect as of a light yellowish amber.

Before the altar, on the left, sits the bishop's chair (the cathedra that gives its name to the cathedral)—inside its own surround with a roof—and with two large lions before it, all this carven out of the same American oak, sanded and varnished and left to look natural, as is all the oak inside the church. Above this main area, far above, sits the painted interior of a dome filled with religious imagery, including (conspicuously) Christos Pancrator with his arms outspread in a gesture of all-embracing strength and protection and love. The cathedral in and out reminded me very much of Byzantine church architecture, undoubtedly extant in close relation. All these data derive from the very gracious lady who had reassured me that I could sit and commune in the church. According to this volunteer worker, some American millionaire has financed the entire religious compound making up the cathedral and associated buildings, and I would guess that he himself derives from Egyptian Coptic descent.

Returning almost at a gallop to the cruise boat, I had just enough time to swim, exercise, dress, rest briefly (but not fall asleep), have lunch, and then go sit in the lobby for the call at 2:00 P.M. to repair to the High Dam and Philae-Agilkia. Looking west from the cruise boat, and north of Elephantine Island, I had noted what resembles an old fortress, apparently halfway up the slope of the nearby low mountains. I asked our new guide (for the afternoon) what it might be, and he identified it as a funerary complex, the Tombs of the Nobles. And as for that squarish domed monument atop a summit south of the complex, he identified it as the shrine of some local Muslim saint or holy man. The double puzzle solved: at last I knew them for what they are.

As a point of reference, Aswan marks the northern end of the First Cataract. The 2:00 P.M. call came, and first we went in minivans to the High Dam, which created Lake Nasser, the world's largest artificial body of water, a virtual inland sea. We reached Lake Nasser over the road that runs on top of the old Aswan Dam (no longer used to store water), built by the British in 1898-1902, once the largest dam in the world, made near totally from Aswan granite, still used to generate electricity for local consumption. Constructed 1960–71, the High Dam contains eighteen times the amount of granite quarried for the Great pyramid of Cheops-Khufu, but even if quite impressive, it does not excite the same kind of wonder. With this dam Egypt creates enough electricity for the entirety of Egypt herself, Jordan, and Israel. Also, the tourist, when visiting the site, understands why the builders did not polish the granite blocks, although perfectly cut and placed in position. The polished surface like an endless mirror would only intensify the sun's rays, especially in the summer, and add immeasurably to the African calescence.

Second, continuing in the minivans, we went to the Temple of Isis on Philae-Agilkia. When construction of the High Dam was finished in 1971, Philae would have vanished beneath the new flood waters, but UNESCO intervened as it did on behalf of Abu Simbel. Between 1972 and 1980 a group of real deconstructionists dismantled the temple complex stone by stone, and rebuilt it on nearby Agilkia. Begun by Ptolemy II (285–246 B.C.E.), it continued in construction under various Ptolemies and then Roman emperors until Diocletian (284–305 C.E.) completed it. The essence of romanticism, this fane has an aura and a glamour that remain unique. In addition to the main temple, the complex has about a dozen or more lesser fanes and other structures, including edifices attributed to Nectanebo, Augustus, Trajan, Hadrian, as well as Diocletian.

If Deir Al-Bahari ranks as the most innovative and stunning temple, and if Karnak as the most gigantic, then "Isis Church" is the most lyrical, individual, and remote (the term comes from *The Faerie Queene,* Book V, Canto VII). This temple has become my own personal favorite, as I sensed in advance that it would, from the descriptions that I have read about it, not to mention the iconic watercolor done of it by David Roberts, a favorite piece of art. Large but not colossal, Philae-Agilkia constitutes in totality the most exquisite ensemble of sacred structures. Overall we spent about an hour and a half at the site. The natural vegetation creates a paradisiacal effect. What a place to camp out overnight! In fact, some Americans have done just that. They had to have a guide with them, and they paid through the nose to do it, but they did it!

Reasonably intact, even if lacking a complete roof like that at

Dendara or Edfu, the Temple of Isis has had her missing roof replaced with a lighter modern equivalent, the skylights letting in a somewhat softened light during the day. Although reconstructed from Philae to Agilkia during 1972–80, the place looks as if it has always existed there, especially the staircases that, in half a dozen locations, go down to the water's edge. Planted after the reconstruction (or preserved where possible), the trees and bushes, the tamarisks and palms, the oleanders and bougainvillea, and other verdure—allowed to flourish between the buildings and around the island's edges—give the finishing touches to this natural setting.

 Something that I did not notice at once, not until the guide pointed it out to me, referred to what many people during the Roman Empire had once regarded as a despised minority: the Christians who, fleeing south, sought refuge here during the early persecutions took over the complex—a somewhat fortressed ensemble—as their home, entire families occupying individual chambers or other spaces. This probably helped the complex to survive, just as the Isis and Horus analogy with Jesus and Mary helped the Christianization of Egypt somewhat earlier. The new inhabitants carved little crosses (rather like the Celtic ones) on the walls here and there throughout the main temple. They also defaced or erased, or tried to do so, some of the older Egyptian images. Faced with so many of them—a hopeless task!—they hardy made a dent.

 What I assumed to be a couple (they hailed from Brazil) was blithely running around the complex from locale to locale, taking photos of each other with their digital cameras, having a grand old time of it. I so enjoyed their enjoyment that I introduced myself and thanked them for their infectious sense of fun. Thereupon, at their express request, I took several photos of them together. So were they a couple? Well, yes and no: She, middle-aged, attractive, svelte, and he, tall, muscular, big-boned but a young man, made a great pair of travelers and revelers together, but as mother and son, not as romantic lovers. Later, at my new hotel in Aswan, I would meet them again. After we returned to the cruise boat, rounding off a very full day of outings, the chefs as magnificent culinary artists prepared for us a superb final dinner, a triumph of *haute nouvelle cuisine*. I had a cocktail to celebrate but did not overdrink or overeat. Pleasantly tired out,

I slept very well that final night aboard that floating palace.

(I see where I am not fulfilling my earlier stated intention to record events more succinctly, probably because I want to remember a lot of relevant facts and nuances. Maybe I'll have better luck recounting the rest of my trip in much less detail. Let us hope.)

Monday, 25 February. After breakfast, while at the front desk, I put £60, the tip for the staff, in an envelope; and I also paid my bar and bottled water bill, £152, thanking the attendant on duty very warmly for the excellent service and amenities provided by all the staff aboard the ship. At 8:30 I met the agent Mahmoud in the lobby and checked out of the *Nile Ruby*, both my bags with me, of course. A driver drove us in a minivan to my new lodging, the Nubanile Hotel, not far away (to the north) but a little inland of the Corniche, very much a budget place, but okay. Still, quite a contrast to the floating palace!

After I checked into the new hotel, we waited for my new guide, Mahmoud's close friend and occasional collaborator Ismaïl. He came soon enough. Neat and well-knit like Mahmoud, but unusually tall (a head higher than I), slender, and elegant, the new guide had specialized in physical culture while in college. Handsome and charming with a great sense of humor, he proved to be an easy-going companion as well as guide. He goes by the name of Smile for Anglophones, has lived in England, and speaks flawless English. My room was not yet ready, and so I checked my big bag behind the counter, keeping my shoulder bag as ever with me, holding as it does all my essentials.

The driver then took Smile and myself to another part of the quay, where we got aboard a canopied and open-sided motor-launch like the one that I took to Philae-Agilkia and then back. Propelled by an affable dark-skinned boy, we first went to (General) Kitchener's Island and the Aswan Botanical Gardens (which he began and initially developed)—a shade-filled garden-park paradise filled with trees almost everywhere. There we leisurely ambulated for an hour or so. Next we went to Elephantine Island, much larger, going around the southern end, where I could not help noticing the huge boulders of granite in and out of the water, as well as (on higher ground) the ruins of Abu, the ancient Aswan (the name Abu means both elephant and ivory). Once past the southern end, we landed at a dock on the southeastern shore, whence we walked up to the Aswan Museum complex, which includes the museum, a small garden, and the ruins of Abu.

Now closed, the museum houses in a handsome, stone, slightly dilapidated Victorian family mansion, which sits up about a story from the ground with a big wide verandah, painted white, wrapping around the front facing east onto the ascent from the landing below. We walked through the small, shady, and rather dusty garden just south of the museum, on into the archaeological site covering several acres or more, including most of the island's southern end, completely exposed to the sun with only a few trees. We lingered first at the Temple of Khnum (very little left except the floor and foundations), and then, on the specially made staircase, at the highest point (staircase and lookout with guardrails), from which the visitor can obtain an all-around view. I noted several smaller Ptolemaic-Roman temples fairly intact, and a great amount of ancient mud-brick construction. Going north from there, we stopped inside a kind of tent where one man was weaving cloth on a hand-loom, and another acted as a salesman. Fascinated by the process, I bought a few small samples of the fabric as gifts for friends.

Continuing north, we walked to the nearest of the two Nubian villages on Elephantine, Koti (south) and Siou (north), but noting the time (early afternoon), I decided to return at once to the mainland in order to get settled in my new hotel room. The boy-man propelled the motor-launch back to the quay, not far from Ferial Gardens across the street from the Coptic Cathedral. (As we had gone by the old museum, the kind curator, unasked, let me use the toilet in the building, but would not accept any tip.) Next Smile and I walked the short distance from the quay to the EgyptAir office to arrange my flight to Abu Simbel on Tuesday, 26 February, rather than by minivan (a very long, cramped ride both ways with few or no restroom stops). The airfare at less than $200 is worth every penny to me in terms of comfort and access to restrooms. Leaving for the Aswan airport early in the morning, I would return to my hotel by early or middle afternoon. Smile then returned me to my hotel, and I gave him the standard tip or more. His guidance and companionship turned out more interesting than those at many of today's tourist sites!

To date, this is the noisiest hotel that I've inhabited (Room No. 203) while in Egypt, located in the noisiest vicinage. My room has a balcony that angles from north to west out toward the very busy street on which the hotel fronts. I finally had time to do my usual half-hour of exercises, which I fit into whatever time slot the day's outing allows me. I'll eat my main meal early evening in the dining room furthest from the lobby. A large swarm of teenage boys on a school trip also inhabit the hotel. They seem to be having a lot of fun, playing pool in the lobby near the elevator, staying up late, riding the elevator at all hours. They seem remarkably similar to American teenagers except for their quietly respectful behavior toward older folk.

After my evening meal I read, jotted a few notes in my notebook, and prepared to go to bed early so I could get up early for my flight via the Aswan airport and EgyptAir to Abu Simbel. However, sometime around 7:15 P.M. I had an unexpected visitor. Someone knocked on the door, I opened it, and there stood Mahmoud, my agent in Aswan, apparently with some special news. I invited him into the room, and we sat facing each other on opposite beds. Abdou in Cairo had received an email from Leo in L.A., and had forwarded it at once to Mahmoud, who considerately was relaying it to me likewise at once. While I was passing my last night on the *Nile Ruby,* Rah died, thus on Sunday, 24 February, sometime between 10:00 and 12:00 at night. As I later discovered by means of a fine and sensitive letter from Leo, Rah received while in the hospital and convalescent home multiple visits from his closest friends (his real relatives), including both Leo and Steven, the latter staying with Rah until around 10:00 during his last two nights and helping him in various ways.

Needless to say, the news was completely unexpected (Rah was ninety-two and with no serious health problems) and hit me with an enormous weight—as people say, "like a ton of bricks." Rah had long since become my best friend, and we had maintained our friendship since May 1961. I maintained my composure, however, and thanked Mahmoud for bringing me the news as soon as he received it. I asked him to convey my thanks as well to Abdou, Leo, and Steve. Mahmoud respectfully waited while I decided (as fast as I could) what I intended to do. Although I might have continued with my four weeks in Egypt as planned, I knew that the settlement of Rah's estate awaited me whenever I returned to L.A., like the proverbial Sword of Damocles. I told Mahmoud that I would finish my third week, and that I would go to Abu Simbel as planned.

Furthermore, I would return to the Luna Hotel in Cairo on the overnight train from Aswan leaving early Tuesday evening, putting me into the capital around mid-morning Wednesday. I would spend Wednesday and Thursday in and around Cairo, and then fly home (going west) on Friday, 1 March. Mahmoud would make the train arrangements and meanwhile inform Abdou, who could then make the flight arrangements by means of Leo, a computer genius, especially at arranging airplane flights, many thanks to him. I owe quite a bit to Mahmoud for handling everything in such a thoughtful and courteous manner. After he left, I found myself much more distraught than I might have anticipated, and wisely took a sleeping aid. It worked very well, and (apart from the usual nocturnal bathroom necessity) I slept quite soundly. I woke up feeling refreshed.

Tuesday, 26 February. I ate an early breakfast in plenty of time for the driver to take me to the airport around mid-morning. The flight to Abu Simbel departed around 10:00 and arrived there at 10:30. Literally sitting high above Lake Nasser, the place lies about 1400 miles from the equator. From the day's prevailing but agreeable warmth, the visitor can imagine how calescent it can become in summer like Deir Al-Bahari. The flight back to Aswan left not at 1:00 P.M. but around 1:30. We arrived back at 2:00, and the driver had me back in the hotel lobby by 2:30. There I met up with Mahmoud for a brief consultation. All was in order. I returned to my room to shower, write notes, take a nap. I had plenty of time.

Abu Simbel? The Great Temple of Ramesses II? Truly colossal, amazing, dumbfounding, mindboggling, etc. (Entrance fee, £95.) I entered both temples "carved out of the living rock" (a cliché phrase but dead-on accurate). Quite a bit of the original colors have survived in the interiors. A film crew was filming a documentary in the smaller but still good-sized Temple of Nefertari, but visitors and crew easily accommodated one another. These monuments allow the visitor to gain a very good concept of what the regular fanes looked like, those not dug out of the bedrock. One walks from the bus or minivan to the site, a little distance. I completely circumnavigated the mound created for these fanes when UNESCO spearheaded the colossal job of removing them (threatened to vanish under the waters of Lake Nasser) to their new location, 1964-68. As I anticipated, visiting Abu Simbel has finally templed me out completely.

I checked out of the Nubanile Hotel (my least favorite) at 6:30, and the driver took me to the train station. The train left on time at 7:00. Soon after I settled in my compartment (No. 13), located about halfway on the connecting corridor in the coach (No. 3), the steward served me a very good meal. After which I read for a while, but soon went to bed once the steward had changed the seat into a bed. I slept rather well, a pleasant surprise, much better than when I took the sleeper train from Cairo to Louqsor. We arrived in Cairo around mid-morning, where Abdou met me and took me back to the Luna Hotel for Wednesday and Thursday nights, the 27th and the 28th. The staff at the front desk—Nasreen and Samirra, who saw me to my former chamber (No. 312)—greeted me warmly. After the noisy Nubanile in Aswan, the Luna seemed all the more the oasis of calm and quietude that I remembered. When Nasreen addressed me with "Welcome back!" it made me feel as if I were coming back home! In a sense I had.

Wednesday, 27 February. An uneventful day for the most part; some exercise and brisk walking. I went back to the Egyptian Museum, and going around the building on the west side, I did not manage to see that cute little cat again, Jungle Kitty as I call him. I pray that he survives all right in an ambiance not kind to stray dogs or cats.

Thursday, 28 February. Abdou drove us back to Saqqara so I could visit the (new) Imhotep Museum, a real beauty, the best small museum that I've encountered in Egypt. I took my time and enjoyed the company of a large group of schoolchildren enjoying a major aspect (pharaoh Djoser and *vizier*-architect Imhotep) of their own country's very early history. From the museum Abdou drove us to the very large mastaba tomb of Ti somewhat to the north or northwest (quite impressive in its own fashion); and then west of there he drove us to the Serapeum near the rest house on the main road. Since he had never gone inside before, Abdou and I visited these catacombs together. Great company!

Almost all the enormous ancient coffins of granite and limestone still stand in place, weighing up to 70 or 80 tons each. The visitor understands at once why they still stand where the ancient Egyptians put them, including one left at the end of the main gallery carved from a single piece of black granite, polished and covered with hieroglyphs. The enormous lid stood separate but not far away. One of the many sons of Ramesses II, Khaemwaset, established the Serapeum on a permanent basis, and at the request of this eminent priest-son (sometimes called the first Egyptologist), his father buried him amid the sacred-bull sarcophagi. This place conforms to my concept of what kind of appearance a gigantic tomb complex should have. The ancients dug the arched tunnels for the galleries out of the bedrock—they are conspicuously wide and high—and constructed both the corridors and the sarcophagus niches on quite a large scale.

I found the subterranean atmosphere marvelously weird and strange, and far more interesting than the beautiful but similar tombs that I visited in the Valley of the Kings all with the same type of hieroglyphic decorations. Everything inside the Serapeum exists on such a large scale that the visitor suffers no claustrophobia. Returning to the Luna Hotel, we ran into the afternoon rush-hour traffic (it began earlier than I would have anticipated). That delayed us by at least an hour or so, but thanks to Abdou's ever skillful driving we finally arrived back in the hotel. That night, as a special treat, in the dining area near the front desk on the fifth floor, Abdou served us each some pea soup that he had made himself, along with some equally tasty rolls. A perfect supper: I needed to eat light so I could sleep soundly during my last night in Egypt. As it happened, I rested long and well. I would need that rest for the seemingly unending flight going back west to L.A.

Friday, 1 March. Before I said goodnight and goodbye to Abdou, I thanked him with the greatest warmth (and through him all his collaborators throughout Egypt) for all the thoughtful and irreplaceable assistance that he (and they) had given me during my three weeks in the country. We said goodbye when we did because as usual Abdou took Friday off as his day of rest. I had already that afternoon given Abdou (as I thought, and he agreed) a very generous bonus; and I had already changed my Egyptian money for American. Of course, you can't really pay people for their good will, but you can pay for the tangible results, the realization of a smooth and comfortable itinerary, made possible by some very kind, very warm, very friendly people.

During another visit, another three weeks, I could sojourn where I did not have time to do so during this first safari just past: Alexandria, St. Catherine's Monastery in the Sinai (built at the command of Justinian and Theodora), the oasis towns in the Western Desert, Abydos, Amarna, etc. Nor would I find it at all disagreeable to revisit some of the sites already visited. Ancient Egypt remains a very powerful enchantress! I had seen most of the major ancient monuments, and I could rest quite content on that score thanks to Abdou and others.

Friday morning I got up at 6:00 A.M., ate breakfast, packed my bags, and waited at the front desk for my ride to the airport. The driver came and got me there with plenty of time for the usual departure procedures. The flight must have left around mid-morning: six hours on EgyptAir, a layover of two or three hours in Munich, then twelve hours on Lufthansa (the single best airline I have ever used) to L.A., arriving on time at 7:45 P.M. As soon as I could clear customs, etc., I took a taxi home, a rare indulgence for me. After that long, long flight I would not balk at such an expense (about $20 with tip). At some point not long after arrival at home, I had fallen asleep at last in my own bed. The house appeared and felt curiously empty without Rah sleeping as usual in his bedroom.

An Interlude in Central America: El Salvador

An Interlude in Central America: El Salvador

I write this memoir of a memorable sojourn in El Salvador at a certain disadvantage. This took place during the entire month of October in 2014. It is now the first part of April 2016, and some two and a half years have gone by. I took no notes at the time, and therefore I must depend on the memory of an eighty-one-year-old man of reduced mentation and faltering recollection, to wit, myself. Nonetheless, I shall make it as accurate as I can, that is, as my failing powers will allow me.

The opportunity came up for me to invest in a property in El Salvador not far from Candelaria de la Frontera near the western border with Guatemala, between that country and the southwestern corridor from Honduras that leads to its narrow coast about fifty miles wide fronting the Pacific Ocean. This corridor borders Nicaragua on the east and south. This small but quite attractive nation measures about fifty miles wide north and south, and about one hundred sixty miles west and east, the length of its own Pacific coast.

The property in which I had invested rates as a hacienda, a multi-crop farm, rather than as a finca, a single-crop one. It has existed as a successful and functioning farm for quite some little time and employs excellent local workers to keep it going. Unless one has labored as an agricultural worker, one has no real concept of just what very hard physical work farming represents, even without the eternal problem of the variable weather all during the growing and then harvesting cycle. One should never underestimate this hard physical labor.

I had invested in the hacienda much less to make money (I pray that I don't lose any!) than much more to have a place to reside in the winter, especially during December through March, and ideally from November through April. As I age, I find that I can tolerate heat much better than unmitigated cold. We might call the hacienda "Jallenco"—after the partnership between the painter Jesse Allen and his assistant, Eric (José) Marenco.

Jesse and Eric purchased the property a few years back, and Eric has proceeded to have several buildings erected on a site not far from the local river, but raised up evidently higher than any foreseeable flood. Most of these new structures now stand completed or almost completed.

Jesse hails originally from Kenya in central Africa, went to school in England, and relocated to California sometime during the 1960s. He currently resides not far from Garberville in Northern California, and moreover in the Redwood Forest (Humboldt County). A native Salvadoreño, Eric resides in Concord, also in Northern California, not far from the San Francisco Bay Area.

We purposed our first month-long sojourn together in El Salvador as a kind of trial or experimental visit so as to determine how the three of us would enjoy living there. Jesse had already visited El Salvador and felt quite comfortable in that ambiance. After various delays we managed to fly from the San Francisco Airport to the one that serves the capital, San Salvador, the chief transportation hub of the country.

As a soccer star, Eric had first come to the United States from his native El Salvador and eventually relocated to the Bay Area, where he met Jesse, recognized him as the remarkable artist that he remains, and became devoted to him as his much-needed assistant. He is in fact indispensable to us in Central America. He speaks and understands fluently both English and, of course, his native Spanish.

Having acquired a considerable gift in languages and their respective bodies of literature at Oxford University in England—he has taught both Italian and French at Stanford University, south of San Francisco—Jesse learned to speak Spanish while residing in the Mission District of the City, and has no problem communicating in that noble tongue. He remains a true polyglot.

As for myself, I studied Spanish for several semesters at UCLA during my four years thereat (overall, 1956-60). Having traveled in both Mexico and Honduras, and after having lived in a Spanish-speaking ambiance, say, for a month, I find that I can speak it well enough to get by, but first I must have real exposure to hearing it spoken and understanding it as it is actually spoken, something of great importance.

Thus all primed and prepared (I had done a little review, using a Spanish grammar), we left California in early October of 2014 and returned home late in that same month, probably around Halloween, and the subsequent Día de Todos los Santos. We flew round trip via

Avianca, leaving in the early evening or so. The flight takes about five hours, and as a routine flight it passes quickly and pleasantly, attended as the passengers are by agreeable and attractive attendants, also bilingual. As usual, drinks and food are served, and one may watch in-flight entertainment (with headphones), or one may simply fall asleep, as many elect to do, a cocktail or two helping in that process.

We landed safe and sound at the airport just outside San Salvador in the very early morning. There one of Eric's closest friends, one Señor Oscar, a charming and simpático gentleman, met us and conveyed us (I think in a station wagon) and our limited luggage to the compound, built around the usual central patio, owned by his mother, la Madre or la Matriarca. (His father had died some time ago.)

Here we would lodge the whole period of our sojourn in El Salvador. This extensive one-story domicile stands about halfway between the capital and Candelaria de la Frontera. Each of us had his own chamber, and we went to bed at once, falling sound asleep. Although the days in October are pleasantly warm, the nights are cool, and one gets under the covers.

When I write of limited luggage, I refer to our personal baggage. We were all traveling light. I never travel with anything more than a medium-sized overnight bag and my smaller shoulder bag. However, as he usually does when returning to his native land, Eric was taking a bunch of stuff back with him, involving maybe half a dozen boxes and bales, all of which needed extensive taping and retaping that he had to do before we could leave from San Francisco. The avoidance of loss and/or mess (e.g., miscellanea dropping out of the bales and boxes inadvertently) dictates this taping and retaping. True, a necessity, but a nuisance as well.

We finally woke up the next morning, but not over-early. We met almost at once la Madre, confined to a wheelchair, and a woman of considerable dignity and age. She had already attained one hundred years, and was one of the few centenarians, or almost centenarians, whom I have met in my lifetime so far. (She was confined to her wheelchair, not because of any particular weakness, but because she had fallen and broken her hip some years before.) Among the almost centenarians I include my favorite French professor, Judd Hubert, who made it through his ninety-ninth birthday on Sunday, 17 January

2016, and then died a week later on Sunday, the 24th.

Jesse had already met la Madre on a previous visit and spoke with her in Spanish in an easy and affectionate way. We also met George, one of Eric's brothers, who also lives in the compound. La Madre made us feel at home at once. One could not help but regard her with awe, affection, and piety, in the ancient Latin or Roman manner. Feeling shy, I rarely spoke with her, uncertain of my Spanish at such short notice.

On the other hand, with the two women who took care of the house, the kitchen, and the cooking while we visited, Doña Miriam and her mother Doña Carolina, I felt no such shyness or compunction, and would attempt speaking Spanish with them. If I made a mistake or could not express myself, they did not correct me so much as they would help me along to find the right word or phrase. I should mention that I have no problem at all in reading or writing Spanish. That morning, as on most mornings, they would make us a solid breakfast with eggs, potatoes, and toast. They also made us other meals, which they would leave for us in the evening. (They came to work every day, residing fairly near at hand.) They also made us good strong Hispanic coffee in the morning. I was and am not accustomed to having people wait on me—I explained that to them, always feeling a little guilty—and always thanked them profusely, even tipping them generously when we departed to return to Northern California.

As far as I can recall, I believe that we went to the hacienda that very first day, Jesse and I both quite eager to have a look-see, particularly at what Eric had wrought there. Eric kept a big van in a kind of garage space just behind the wooden gate leading into the compound, and Eric now drove us to the property. After half an hour or less we arrived at the hacienda. I suffered no disappointment. As a multi-crop farm it looked as if the farm workers had it all in good order, the crops and fields arranged in even furrows. As soon as we parked, we walked a little distance to where the buildings were standing, some completed, some in the process of being completed in various stages, all with red ceramic tile roofs.

The completed structures included the storage building, and next to it the caretakers' house, a relatively small but handsome building. The caretakers were already living there with their little daughter.

Made out of red brick, the residence has a beautiful arcaded surround or verandah. The then uncompleted main house loomed much larger, with a big practical kitchen (actually the main room) leading to two suites, each with spacious bedroom and bathroom. (The construction workers had not yet installed the windows.) Next to the main house loomed the even larger studio, where Jesse would be doing his paintings. The ceilings here rose even higher than those in the main house as dictated by the hot summers; high ceilings like these really function to keep the lower part of the chambers cool in the hottest weather.

Since my visit Eric has added a spacious guest-house but not yet finished. There was also already built a kind of roofed well-structure, not large but with four square corner pillars, the well filled with good clean water and topped by a stainless-steel tank beneath the roof; the tank was also filled with water for immediate domestic use. We met the caretakers, a young couple, thus already in residence to keep an eye on the buildings as a safety factor, or arrangement, a wise precaution. We also met the woman architect, who insisted on acting as her own builder or contractor. Eric later realized that he should not have allowed this. Among other buildings she had constructed the studio incorrectly, cheating on the foundation and the materials and not paying the construction workers in full *comme il faut*. Thus these unfortunate circumstances forced Eric to discharge her and will force him to make some expensive and essential repairs later.

Following this first and extended inspection of the structures, Eric guided us down to the river, to a spot already a favorite with him, as it would become for us all as a threesome. We had brought some light folding chairs with us. Setting them up and sitting comfortably, we loitered there for at least half an hour, utterly enjoying the ambiance and its beauty. Several ceiba trees, all very large, but one a giant several hundred years old, distinguished the river bank where we sat above the stream.

Apart from their off-white or light gray trunks, here and there around their girth, say, halfway down their trunks, what appear like ridged buttresses really make these trees stand out distinctly. I had already noticed trees like these in Honduras, but nothing as large as these examples. Trees that look similar also grow in Southeast Asia, but although tropical or semi-tropical, I doubt that they are related. I do not pose as an arboreal expert, Great Goddess forbid.

In this way went our first visit, but only the first of many visits that we would make to the hacienda during our sojourn in El Salvador. As I have already found them whether in Mexico or in Central America, the Hispanic people everywhere I went, above all in the rural areas, appeared friendly, solicitous, and genial. What a pleasure to have them as companions! Apart from Nicaragua, Central America seems politically stable, reasonably safe and secure, meaning Belize, El Salvador, Honduras, Costa Rica, and Panama.

I can't speak for Guatemala, nor having spent any significant period there, apart from passing through it once en route to a day and a night in Yucatán, after visiting at Copán in Honduras. El Salvador strikes me as a model country: the people use American dollars (no need to change currency as often happens when journeying abroad), and English is the second language. Most educated and professional people speak very good English (probably better than many Americans!), making it much easier for gringos to communicate. A little Spanish will indeed go quite a long way.

In addition to near daily trips to the hacienda (or thus it seems in retrospect), Eric sometimes drove us to other places of interest, such as the Pacific seashore, when Oscar and his family in an extra vehicle accompanied us. The celebrated Copán in Honduras lies only about sixty miles away to the northnortheast as the bird flies, that is, from Candelaria. I sojourned in Copán in the latter 1980s for about a week, staying in the town of Copán Ruinas [*sic*], also known (I believe) as San José de Copán.

The ruins, no longer quite so ruinous, but restored in large part, appear almost completely excavated and present an astonishing spectacle, most of it freed of the tropical verdure. El Salvador has no site or ancient city comparable to Copán, but it seems to have several very well-preserved Mayan pyramids, one of which I managed to inspect up close, albeit briefly, during one of our vehicular jaunts. These vestiges of long-gone grandeur impress me as much as anything I have witnessed in Southeast Asia, including Angkor in Cambodia or Ayutthaya north of Bangkok.

In retrospect I must record in profound gratitude that Eric as our general cicerone and "protector" took excellent care of Jesse and myself, acting always with solicitude and fastidious consideration. Knowing my predilection for rum and Coke (or rum and Pepsi), for an occasional cocktail thereof, he kept us well supplied with dark rum, Coca-Cola, and ice. Back at his mother's compound, a group of us would sit on occasion around a big circular table in another part of the multifold patio and imbibe one or more cocktails, hanging out in luxurious idleness. These little trips to the hacienda, and sometimes around the country, made up the pattern of our days while in Honduras and while based at the compound (not far from the little city of Santa Ana), where we spent most of our other time, our temporary home away from home.

It all turned out as a satisfying, low-key, but genuine adventure. On one occasion we passed an agreeable hour with the then major of Candelaria, one Janet Ribeira, not just an adroit politician, but also a strikingly handsome woman of sophisticated charm. We could claim her in a sense as a neighbor and a potential ally since the hacienda lies only fifteen or twenty minutes away from Candelaria by van or car. Both Jesse and I became as happy as Eric with the farm, no less than with the progress that he was making with the construction of all the new structures at the main residential site.

It appears that Eric had inherited from his father several apartment buildings, which he sold. With the money from the sale he purchased the hacienda, and consulting with one or more architects he began laying out the new buildings. Jesse and he had already concocted the overall plan for the property; and Jesse, who commands excellent prices for his unique paintings, went in with Eric on the new place with an equal financial standing.

Subsequently I joined in with them, investing almost the same amount of money that each of them had furnished. I must say in keen admiration and appreciation that Eric as our man on the ground had assumed quite an onerous task in doing what he has managed to accomplish. Overall he has discharged his task with determination and perseverance, despite all the stresses and strains that such a huge task imposes on he who achieves it.

Not being directly involved, apart from my investment, no less than apart from my month-long sojourn in El Salvador during October of 2014, I can only applaud Eric on how he has handled everything. I look forward eagerly to my future periods of residence in legended Central America! Oh, the poetry of those Maya ruins!

A Trip to Hawaii and Micronesia

An idiosyncratic itinerary to Hawaii's Big Island, and then to Pohnpei and Kosrae, mid-April to mid-May (actually 13 April to 8 May) 2015. (A travel report.)
—Donald Sidney-Fryer

North Auburn, California
June 2015.

A Trip to Hawaii and Micronesia

Sometime after I moved in with James (Eldon) Patterson on 23 February 2014, and before housemate James for cogent reasons of health decided to retire (which he did on 16 March 2015), I proposed as a special treat for James and myself that he and I should travel to some exotic realm or realms together. It would make a special retirement gift from D.S.F. to James, and I would take care of all or most of the expenses, the travel by aircraft, car rentals, lodging, meals in restaurants, etc. And I did so take care of them!

I had proffered him a choice, either Southeast Asia (with Bangkok in Thailand as our base, and with the major outing on into Cambodia to visit Angkor via access town Siem Riep) or, say, Hawaii and Micronesia, the latter for the megalithic ruins at Nan Madol and Leluh, respectively, on Pohnpei and Kosrae. James chose the latter, hence a custom-tailored itinerary, via Hawaiian and United Airlines. This turned out much more expensive than the established and well-worn route from California to Bangkok and back. Still, I myself would at least see something of Nan Madol and Leluh, which I had long desired to do.

Essential to our plans is James's abilities as a professional driver, as well as a private one: he has driven both taxis and big rigs (the latter for the last eight years), and indeed has just retired from the big rigs. He had already visited Oahu twice, but had always wanted to see the Big Island (more properly called Hawaii) with its unique terrain, volcanos, and generally undeveloped condition. I had never visited Hawaii before at all, but once I found myself in a private (rented) house outside the little town of Pahoa, some ten miles or so south of Hilo, I was very pleased that James had chosen the Big Island, and then Micronesia.

On Monday, 13 April, we left our residence, the dear old funky farmhouse, at 6:30 A.M., our great friend and landlord David Anello driving us to the Sacramento (ahem, International) Airport. We had plenty of time to leave on our pleasant and routine flight at 9:45 A.M. via Hawaiian Airlines. After some five hours we arrived in Honolulu safe and sound in the early afternoon with enough time to catch our inter-island shuttle to Hilo on the Big Island. The shuttle took about an hour, and although pleasant and routine, the flight on the much smaller airplane turned out as the most cramped and uncomfortable, if not claustrophobic, aircraft ride that I have ever endured.

I announced the fact quite loudly to the flight attendants when we left the plane, and I thanked them for attending to us. I like close and cozy but not cramped and claustrophobic, much harder on James at sixty-two (who has the broad shoulders and neck of an ox!) than on me at eighty! I could hardly wait to get off that consarned plane around mid-afternoon in Hilo, ugh! The experience on the inter-island shuttle left James (who had not flown for about a decade or so) quite negatively impressed. I agreed!

We went at once to the car rental booths or counters outside the terminal building. We never had to wait on any checked luggage, since we both traveled with overnight bag or backpack, plus a smaller pack or shoulder bag. Renting a four-door sedan from Hertz, James drove us with all due speed and safety to the rental house north of the little town of Pahoa, which Joyce Tagorda owns (but lives in Tennessee) and handles with the help of a local agency (which also manages the cleaning between guests), and with the help of a neighbor across the street who looks after the property otherwise. As indicated in advance, we found the key to the front door, and the garage-door hand-control, in the mailbox. While I went in through the front door, James entered through the garage. All was well and in order.

The rental home can easily house a big family or other large group with room to spare: a large spacious family mansion with high ceilings everywhere, a benediction given the climate—a front vestibule opening into or onto a gigantic hallway (two stories tall) with a broad and elegant staircase going up to the second floor, and a kind of mezzanine space that can sleep two or more persons (by means of some sofas that easily change into beds), and thus on the same level as the upstairs bedrooms and bath. The main hallway on the main level also opens up into the living room proper, dining room, and a big spacious kitchen with convenient granite-topped "island" (counter) for eating or food preparation.

The master bedroom and huge bathroom sit on the main floor, plus another large bedroom and bath off the big open area. One can enter the house either by the front door or the three-car garage accessible from the back or lateral hallway. But the really big surprise takes the shape of an enormous family room with windows opening onto the back yard, a chamber with a very high ceiling extending upward more than two stories, and thus overtopping the rest of the domicile. A person can look from the mezzanine balcony both up and then down into this refreshingly gigantic space. The family `room contains the usual big-screen TV, sound system, radio, etc., perfect for a large group, especially a big family.

With the aid of two close friends using the Internet, James had shopped around to find this house, reasoning wisely that we would fare better and cheaper by renting a house and making our own meals (when we would not eat out in restaurants) than by staying in some rather more expensive hotel. We bought groceries at once (including beer and spirits) and later supplemented them as we needed. I believe, though, that we ate out that evening and went to bed early. The trip, in addition to getting settled in at the house, had made us good and tired. I had not slept well the night before our flight, but certainly managed to get a good night's rest that first night in Hawaii. With our base and food secured, we could commence discovering and exploring the next morning.

Hawaii turns out exactly as described by many natives or outside travelers. The landscape remains lush, tropical, geologically varied, and very green, with few or no sandy beaches. Unlike California, now in its third or fourth year of drouth, Hawaii has abundant water, as do most ocean islands in the tropical zone. It rains a helluva lot, and with the comfortable temperatures (mostly in the 80s) and pleasant humidity, the air or atmosphere seems unusually soft and almost ideal in how it feels on the (human) skin.

We had hoped the night before to begin to discover and explore the island, but we found that we still needed to get more supplies, including more food and other basics. And so we devoted our first full day in Hawaii to doing just that. Not particularly thrilling, but practical and necessary. We also got to know a few of the nearest restaurants whether for breakfast or for supper, such as Ken's House of Pancakes and the Coconut Grill.

After breakfast we shopped at the local Walmart in Hilo, a very large and comprehensive emporium, the first time that I have patronized a store of this chain. No wonder people flock to the Walmarts at convenient malls. They can do all or most of their shopping (including food) under one roof. Walmart sells their goods at reasonable or inexpensive prices. The Hawaiian salespeople could not have acted more agreeably. What great people!

Besides some basics we bought inexpensive postcards, souvenirs, maps, sightseeing booklets, etc.

As we laid the foundation for our two-week sojourn, that first full day turned into something long and rather tiring. We returned home for lunch and then a nap. Later we went out again to visit an exceptional used bookstore in Pahoa, following which we drove north to Hilo again to visit another exceptional used bookstore. Before returning home, we ate on the coast near Hilo at the famous (first-rate) Seaside eatery, specializing in fish and other seafood, which turned out exceptional. The eatery even grows its own fish in special salt-water pens. However, neither drinks nor food came cheap, and James did not like his choice.

When we finally got to bed around midnight, I had learned several salient facts about Hawaii concerning which friends had already warned us. Nothing—food, dry goods, etc., not to mention restaurants—comes cheap in the Hawaiian islands. I thought on my return from Southeast Asia that the U.S. mainland was expensive, but Hawaii is even more so. The one chief grace and consolation of the islands: Hawaii is indeed gorgeous. Given the high prices, I doubt that I shall ever return, even if I am enjoying my current sojourn with James.

The rented house lies on the windward or rainy side of the island, which as on all the other islands receives most of the rain, quite an abundant rain, an understatement. The western or Kona coast lies on the leeward or arid side of the island, where the famous Kona coffee grows, requiring irrigation, even if the western coast does receive some precipitation, but nothing like what falls on the windward side. The two broad and massive mountains Mauna Kea and Mauna Loa, potentially active volcanos that could explode at any time, physically dominate the island. You can observe them easily from almost any part of the landmass.

As I lay in bed after that first full day, before I fell asleep, I reflected with some satisfaction that at least we had prepared well for the main part of our exotic sojourn and had learned the basic layout of the land. Maps and guidebooks would assist further as we negotiated the terrain when finally the next day we could begin discovery and exploration.

James makes breakfast and supper—he's a good cook. I make lunch, usually a big salad. As always, I prefer small portions for breakfast and supper, avoiding much meat at night, especially beef, harder to digest at night for an older person. On occasion we go to some eatery nearby. I prefer the humble Coconut Grill to the fancy Seaside near Hilo. At the grill I can get almost the same thing, whether food or cocktail, but cheaper and faster. We shall try some other seafood place, say, at Pahoa. Apart from tourist sites, here are a few revelations that we have made on our own at once, or that we have had from friends based on their hands-on experience.

Whenever America takes over any place, the prices go up. Our capitalism does not always improve our exotic territories. As James puts it pithily, that's the way that the U.S. does it. It changes a paradise into a shithole and charges more money for it! We understand that Oahu (Honolulu) has become the L.A. of these islands, having undergone total development. Yet the real natives, whenever and wherever I encounter them, remain warm and friendly. Amazing! Despite everything negative that has happened to them since contact with Caucasians, including annexation, they and their culture have managed to survive. Their culture at present is undergoing a genuine renaissance, and that includes their liquid, many-voweled language, ideal for singing, even more so than Italian. Again, amazing!

Hawaiian music! I had no idea how varied and evolved it has long since become. In fact, I have rarely heard it until I came to the big island. The singers have beautiful voices, unlike so many of the pop singers on the mainland, whether rock, folk, or country-western. We have been playing near exclusively the Hawaiian music that we can get easily on the auto's radio when we drive someplace. The music seems eternally soothing and positive, and yet not monotonous. Among the current singers who stand out, I notice a certain Robi with mellifluous voice and delivery. Although not Hawaiian, she teaches Hawaiian as a professor and speaks it fluently.

Finally, but finally, after our flight from Sacramento to Honolulu, and then from there to Hilo, after settling in at our spacious rental house, and after going to various markets and other shops for supplies of booze and food (including wine for our meals), we had finished all the preparations for our sojourn. Thus we could discover and explore the natural features of this latest and largest island of the Hawaiian archipelago. Hallelujah! Today we visited from 8:00 A.M. until 1:30 P.M. the Hawaii National Volcanoes Park, which like most national parks the authorities maintain in an exemplary manner despite budget cuts or lack of sufficient funding.

We spent some considerable time at the park's visitor center, so we could grasp the local vulcanism in all its depth and range. Now do I understand why the biggest island has not undergone much development. Mauna Kea and Mauna Loa might erupt at any time and send their lava flows almost anywhere, destroying anything in their path—town, village, city, isolated installation. James drove us next southeast along the Chain of Craters Road all the way to the southern coast to another visitor center, and to the rocky cliffs 40 or 50 feet above the ocean. He bought some quality souvenirs, but I purchased only a slender book (a trade paperback of 100 pages) about Liliuokalani (1838-1917), Hawaii's last monarch.

Some few years back I had seen a documentary about this queen on TV, which covered some aspects of her reign, but I had read very little about her and her struggle to keep her far-flung realm independent and free from annexation. The U.S. could have handled the latter with a bit more delicacy and finesse. Instead of deposing her and annexing the islands, the U.S. might have made Hawaii a protectorate, outwardly maintaining the status quo. Through all the vicissitudes her people remained loyal to her. Her remarkable and forthright character stands out in the historical record. Reading about her life, I cannot withhold my sympathy, nay, tears of compassion, on behalf of her struggle against the behemoth that is the U.S. I suffered no great surprise when I discovered that a group of American businessmen conspired against the queen and engineered both her downfall and the annexation. She remains an admirable figure, whereas the businessmen have become despicable.

The Volcanoes Park affords an extraordinary geological experience: the various calderas, the old lava fields, and so forth, remind the visitor of the awesome power of Mother Nature versus the puniness of *Homo sapiens,* the greatest of her upstart offspring! We visited the Jaggar Museum last, which lies north of the chief visitor center. The big island comes in at around 4000 square miles, a thousand miles less than Connecticut. That might seem small as part of the continental U.S., but not quite so small as an island amid the vast Pacific Ocean!

This first day of freedom from preparation, free to roam and explore, furnished the model for most of our days on the big island, our days of discovery and exploration facilitated by James's expert driving of the rental car. We returned home for a late light lunch, a needed time in the bathroom, and then a nap. James made our supper, just as he had made our breakfast. As usual, I did the cleaning up. Once again we went to bed early. During our first full day in Hawaii, Tuesday, 14 April, still one of preparation for our sojourn, we had visited Hilo Bay Books, which had reminded me of a miniature Acres of Books (Long Beach, California). On Wednesday, the 15th, we had visited the Volcanoes Park, and for Thursday, the 16th, we had planned to visit the orchid farm belonging to a friend, John Mungo, of another friend, Brent, friend to James since high school. But we got our directions wrong—the orchid farm lies not far from the rental house—and phoned Mungo, explained our error, and arranged to visit him the next day, getting better directions.

We decided on the spot to visit the town of Kona-Kailua, where Kona Bay Books is located (affiliated with Hilo Bay Books), which James wanted to explore. Fine! To reach the dry Kona coast on the west we drove on the Saddle Road across the immense Saddle Region between Maunas Kea and Loa, an area of former lava flows, desolate, awesome, rather monotonous, and with minimum verdure. We reached the attractive town of Kona-Kailua and the bookstore, where we met the enchanting used bookstore owner, a brilliant and articulate woman called Chris (she owns both Kona Bay and Hilo Bay Books). This much larger store bore an even greater resemblance to Acres of Books, which Chris had known directly. She had once managed a bookstore not far from Long Beach, a bookstore that later changed into an Upstart Crow, one of a small chain. The name refers to William Shakespeare. We must have eaten lunch somewhere, but I can't recall, and I failed to note it in my journal.

While in Kona-Kailua, looking east, we had noticed a high extensive slope rising east of the town almost at once, the slope likely belonging to Mount Hualalai as a distant part. That peak rose over 2500 feet some ten miles eastnortheast of the little city. The slope formed a rare gradual terrain free from the lava flows of Maunas Kea and Loa, a terrain that people had terraced for many private homes and gardens, an ideal place for domestic development custom-built.

Despite the awkward colon and bladder condition of notable discomfort now going into its second month, I managed to enjoy today's adventure. We visited John Mungo's orchid farm, which must cover about two football fields, mostly topped with netting that keeps away the birds and reduces the impact of sun and rain. Strange but pleasant to wander far afield amid the orchids growing everywhere. We all got wet as it lightly rained, and as John guided us amid the orchid-growing plots. We went inside for a while. I had not slept that well the night before, and feeling tired and sleepy, I lay down on a bed in the billiard annex (a separate part of the residence) and, covered over with a bunch of sheets, rested and slept for a little. Meanwhile John and James harvested orchids for later pick-up. After we all returned to the main house (where his son was sleeping, a computer whiz and night person), we smoked and then made our departure. John seemed a fine host and companionable person. We would return on another occasion.

Before we left, John turned us on with something called noni juice, made from the local noni fruit, whose flesh and juice have a somewhat cheeselike flavor, not unpleasant. We then visited the man who makes the juice and a powder derived from the fruit. It seems to help gastro-intestinal problems like mine, and so I purchased capsules of the powder. James himself bought both juice and a big bag of powder for later encapsulation. We returned home for lunch. James leaves at 3:00 P.M., and will pick Mike Green up at 4:00 P.M., coming over from Honolulu to the Hilo airport. They should arrive at 5:00 or 5:30 P.M., depending on the local rush-hour traffic.

On Saturday, 17 April, Mike (a true hero) spent much of the morning (using his laptop computer) in arranging our lodging for Guam, Pohnpei, and Kosrae, something that James and I had foolishly neglected. The evening previous, before arriving home, James and

Mike had gone shopping for wine and more provisions. We had eaten Chinese take-out food, purty good and worth the money (not bad) for the trouble that it had saved us because we did not need to prepare a meal. Mike remains a great comfort as friend and companion. He adds much joy to the household. We remained at home for much of Saturday, but went out for lunch at Pahoa Fish and Chips: better than any that I have had in the U.K. Later under Mike's guidance we went out again for our first genuine Hawaiian meal in an Hawaiian restaurant. Good, especially the lau-lau, but too much pork and starch for my taste, not to mention greasy fat.

Another quiet time on Sunday, 19 April. We left late morning to get Mike to his plane at high noon to return to Oahu. All goes well, and we return home after more shopping for basics. An added person at meals uses up more supplies. On Monday, 20 April, after breakfast at Ken's House of Pancakes, we began mid-morning our circuit of the island on the so-called Belt Road. This does not make a perfect circuit everywhere (near the shore) because it does not and cannot traverse the Volcanoes Park, but goes around it on the north. Starting out, we went north into the Kohala peninsula before heading south again to Kona-Kailua and Kona Bay Books. Early afternoon we had become hungry again and visited a special eatery (in Kainaliu) recommended by Mike and other friends, Annie's Burgers. There we ate an excellent meal of classic cheeseburgers and special French fries, all superbly prepared. After which, and my inevitable trip to the bathroom, we continued our circuit around the island, south, east, north (around the northern part of Volcanoes Park), and then east and southeast to our temporary home north of Pahoa. On Tuesday, 21 April, we went back to John Mungo's orchid farm, as enjoyable as ever. What an exotic experience! On Wednesday, 22 April, we stayed at home. I wrote all day (my journal and the extra chapters for my autobiography) and ate at home except for our supper, when we returned to Pahoa Fish and Chips, ate half of our meal there, and then returned home with the other half, saved for later consumption.

During our earlier trip to the Kohala peninsula we had only touched the southern area, but now we wanted to explore the major part. Which we did! Beautiful, pastoral, and rolling countryside of lavish verdure except for the peninsula's eastern coast, just as verdant, but impenetrable by motor vehicle. After our return home, we went back down to the little town of Pahoa to eat at Luquin's Mexican restaurant. Quite exotic to consume a typical Mexican meal in a little Hawaiian town!

On Friday, 24 April, we remain at home, pack up, etc., to continue our itinerary elsewhere. I continue scrivening on my journal and the extra chapters for my autobiography. We leave for Guam on Saturday, 25 April. After making sure that the rental is in good shape (I have a $300 security deposit to return to me), we depart late morning from Hilo for Honolulu and then depart from there sometime in the afternoon. All goes as planned or scheduled. The flight from Honolulu turns out long and (as ever) very tiring. Because of the International Date Line, we arrive in Guam on Sunday, the 26th, even if it stays the very same physical day! Weird! Apparent paradox, but that's it: apparent paradox only. People have been reminding me when air travel could seem a real pleasure. Pray tell, when was that? I can't quite remember.

Due to our own miscalculation (not Mike Green's), we get hung up on Guam from Sunday through Tuesday (26, 27, 28 April), thus reducing our time on Pohnpei to two nights and three days. Elana Johnson, working at the counter for United, saves our unenlightened selves, so that we have lost time but no money. Guam, which played a major role in the American takeover of the Pacific "theatre" during World War II, seems to be a high-end shopping destination for mostly well-off young Japanese tourists, but is otherwise inane and insipid. Our Grand Plaza Hotel, family-style geared to the Japanese, sits just north of a long line of what might appear to be a series of elegant fortresses or banks, only two stories or so tall, some with gleaming metal portals (which look as if they could withstand an armed assault), but which turn out to be secular temples devoted to the worship of the twin gods of High Fashion and Mammon but going under the names of Louis Vuitton, Gucci, Prada, Yves St. Laurent, etc.

Finally we fly from Guam on Tuesday, 28 April (per Guam time, Wednesday, 29 April), and land after five hours on Pohnpei on the same day and date (again, the apparent confusion stems from the International Date Line between Guam and Pohnpei). We make it to our Mangrove Bay Hotel. So, upon further thought and calculation, we actually have three nights and four not-quite-full days on this fascinating island of extraordinary beauty. (We shall depart from Pohnpei for Kosrae on Friday, 1 May.) The circa 170-square-mile, verdure-clad, mountainous island exceeds my expectations. Through a local travel agency we hire a local guide, Mario, to take us as soon as possible to the megalithic ruins of Nan Madol on the east or eastsoutheast coast. On Wednesday, 29 April, he drives us to Nan Madol; it takes us about an hour to get there on the two-lane road. Mario, a lovely man and guide, has taken many people to the gigantic site about five miles long east and west, and two miles north and south.

The diagrams of the site in the guidebooks are misleading. They seem to limn a vast open area of stone islets with canals or other waterways, promising a veritable Venice of the Pacific. Otherwise mangrove trees and other heavy-duty vegetation utterly cover the site. It would require millions of dollars to clear the site of all the verdure, otherwise inaccessible to the average visitor. For that reason Mario chaperones us to the only open site at the eastern end of Nan Madol, to wit, Nan Dowas, a typical edifice built up with basalt logs, and surely impressive. The natives should never have abandoned the city!

The visitors pay several small fees to the local people who own the land, the access to Nan Dowas. The seriously interested individual could visit more of the gigantic site of Nan Madol, but would need to make serious preparations and to wear serious gear, boots, waders, etc., and would need to hire several local people for several weeks. Otherwise, a major disappointment in terms of easy accessibility.

On Thursday, 30 April, Mario drives around other areas of the island, including the administrative center in Kolonia, the capital, which has a surprising number of full-fledged embassies. En route back to our hotel Mario stops at the Woodcarvers Village for an extended visit. We had wanted to shop here for several small souvenirs (such as we can carry in our bigger bag or luggage, with our clothing wrapped around them for protection). I bought several small wooden sculptures, and James a small number of necklaces whose center pieces looked as if carved out of ivory, but actually out of a species of hard nut, made to resemble tiny dolphins, fancy fish-hooks, etc. The prices appear reasonable but not giveaways. I personally would rather overpay than the opposite. We did not cheat the carvers, an unusually so-ber bunch of men, unsmiling unlike most Polynesians. We respected their sobriety, which gave the carvers enormous dignity.

After our too brief sojourn we depart on Friday, 1 May, around noon, from Pohnpei, via the awful United Airlines and arrive on Kosrae an hour or so later after covering some 400 miles on the island-hopper jet plane. During the week from Friday, 1 May, to Friday, 8 May, we shall overnight at the excellent Pacific Treelodge Resort, owned and managed by husband and wife team Mark Stephen (from Tennessee) and Maria Fenelli (from Ancona near Rome). Here we have our own cottage (one of half a dozen) with two big comfortable beds. We mostly eat at Bully's, the resort restaurant and bar, built out over the inner water area extending out from the mangrove trees that give the lodge its name, a mere stone's throw from the ocean beach to the east. Bully's provides pretty good food and service as well as alcoholic drinks. The women waiting on us could not be sweeter and more obliging; they speak excellent English! Indeed, as on Pohnpei, so on Kosrae: one could not find sweeter, warmer, and more amiable folk. How easy to be pleasant with such pleasant people! We rented from Mark and Maria one of their rental cars on several different days in order to visit certain places of historical and other interest, above all the Leluh Ruins on Leluh Island just to the southeast of our resort. This compound and enclosure made of basalt logs à la Nan Dowas, where the royalty and nobility once resided, remains quite impressive, even if overgrown à la Nan Madol; it needs once again extensive care and renewed attention.

Although smaller at 42 square miles than Pohnpei at 168 square miles or so, Kosrae stays as lush and green as the larger isle. Both islands have barrier reefs that protect them from typhoons and tsunamis, which rarely visit these last islands; rather, those phenomena appear to start in or around this oceanic area and seldom trouble Pohnpei and Kosrae. We walk or drive as need or inclination indicates. One walks with care on these only two-way paved roads, which usually do not run far from the ocean shore, if not right next to it. In short, our sojourn on Kosrae turns into an uncommon and peaceful idyll thanks to Mark and Maria. It rains even more here than in Hawaii and Guam, and these two islands, it bears repeating, receive some 14 or 16 feet of rainfall per year, making them two of the wettest places on the planet. The native people here have somehow survived the incursions of Europeans and Americans, with all their exotic diseases but at great cost to their numbers. By the time that Christian (Protestant) missionaries arrived in 1852, literally to save the natives, the overall population had reduced from around 5,000 to only 300 persons or so!

After breakfast on our last day, Friday, 8 May, the bill for food, lodging, drinks, car rental, and so forth, for our week at the resort, came to $1,113.75. With tips the overall cost went up to and a bit beyond $1200, what I had expected. Not bad, everything (including convenience) considered. (The Hertz rental car cost us $600 for two weeks in Hawaii.) Remember, dear reader, that almost everything must come onto the island by ship, and the owners order everything they need a month or more in advance. We also ate on occasion at the restaurants inside the two other chief resorts, Kosrae Village Ecolodge and Kosrae Nautilus Resort. We thanked all the staff at Pacific Treelodge for their service and good will, and I gave our six chief servers a $20 bonus each, in addition to the earlier tips that we had both given them. They appreciated our appreciation! On several occasions during a quiet evening Sepi (one of the chefs, and a lovely woman), aided by her three-string ukulele, and in collaboration with some of the younger women regaled us with a lovely concert of native songs beautifully sung and harmonized, but not overprojected in an operatic manner. A real treat!

The mercifully routine flight back to Sacramento, however long and tedious (especially the layovers in terminals one after another) went well, apart from the extreme annoyance caused by the two or three security checks on Kosrae, Kwajalein, and Majuro. Four of the eight and a half hours from Kosrae to Honolulu, we spent mostly waiting on the security people to do and finish their job thanks to Dick Cheney's infamous Department of Homeland Security. However, the rest of the trip from Honolulu to San Francisco to Sacramento went forward without any undue delays, just the usual ones. I shall do my utmost to avoid flying on United Airlines ever again; they no longer even serve meals—the passenger may purchase instead a boxed "snack."

What a relief when James and I, picked up and brought back by

James's daughter Sierra and her partner Cole, finally found ourselves ensconced back home in the late afternoon or earliest evening! It took us the usual several days or so to recover from the always ghastly return flight home. But we did! How ineffable to rest and relax away from the hordes of airline passengers, to settle in at home away from those unending airline terminals! Otherwise we had enjoyed a great good vacation.

Amen, amen, amen.

N.B. One event that I failed to record anent our sojourn on Kosrae, I shall chronicle briefly here, an idyll of idylls. James and I with a few other people signed up for the harbor cruise that always happens (if enough sign up for it) on Thursday evening, as did our own, on 7 May 2015. This takes place on the inner waterway from north of Treelodge to south of Leluh Island. Late in the afternoon, at 5:00 P.M., "Captain" Mark with his young son Oceano (six or so) met us on the dock at the south end of Bully's bar and restaurant. There he had waiting for us a fair-sized motor launch onto which we all filed. Mark started the engine and off we went, refreshed on occasion by some spray as Mark maneuvered the boat. We went all the way south of Leluh Island and came to rest almost opposite the entrance to Leluh Harbor on the east. Here we could feel and see the great surge of the ocean coming in from that wide entrance.

Mark attached our launch with a sturdy rope to his thirty-foot sailboat that he has anchored there. Picturesque and verdure-clad Mount Finkol rose up to its height of 630 metres to the southwest of where we had come to rest. Once in place, we ate sushi and imbibed beer, an interesting combination. After the sun had set, and after much good conversation among the six of us as the convivial guests, our good captain unattached the launch from the sailboat, and in the darkening twilight we returned to Bully's, following an altogether delectable outing. Once we landed, I sought out the kitchen staff, and thanked them for the sushi, expertly prepared.

Time-Line Night at Beyond Baroque

Time-Line Night at Beyond Baroque, 681 Venice Blvd., Venice, California, 90291: Saturday, 8 December 2012, c. 7:00–10:00 P.M., a personal report by an humble participant.

Concerning the celebration of *Visions and Affiliations: A California Literary Time Line: Poets and Poetry, 1940-2005* (but actually extending beyond those dates both before and after in a number of cases), in two volumes by Jack Foley (Pantograph Press, Oakland, Calif., 2011), the celebration as hosted by Jack and Adelle Foley.

An evening of poetry, not of poets, featuring (in alphabetical order): Will Alexander, Adelle Foley, Michael C. Ford, Kate Gale, Dana Gioia, Pegarty Long, Suzanne Lummis, Sarah Maclay, Estelle Gershgoren Novak, Harry Polkinhorn, Jerome Rothenberg, Donald Sidney-Fryer, Timothy Steele, David St. John, Amy Uyematsu, and Paul Vangelisti.

For whatever compelling reasons, one or more poets advertised as featured could not appear at the event, and Jack Foley read their selections himself, thus covering for them.

This report is dedicated to Kenneth W. Faig, Jr. of Glenview, Illinois, for his kind and eloquent interest in the oeuvre and career of Donald Sidney-Fryer, still sometime known as the Last of the Courtly Poets. An eminent scholar and Lovecraftian, Kenneth has sustained this interest (among a great many) over many years.

Accompanied by my great and good friend John Miller of Glendale, California, and driven to the event by him in his car, I showed up at Beyond Baroque around 7:00 P.M. As the current director of this artistic-literary private (and non-profit) institution, Richard Modiano greeted us at the door, where we also met Mike Sonksen, a young poet, scholar, tour guide, and lecturer, among other accomplishments. At Modiano's request the featured poets entered the performing hall (a small auditorium) and thus assembled there in advance as they arrived. Meanwhile a good-sized audience (probably half a hundred persons) was gathering inside and outside the front door. They entered the hall sometime after 7:30 P.M.

Beyond Baroque occupies the old Venice City Hall (on the north side of Venice Blvd.), an attractive, rather Mission-style structure, endowed with basement, several stories, and even a tower. The auditorium, the equivalent of a medium-sized recital or concert hall in a college music school, makes a pretty good venue for spoken-word performances with or without microphones. By the time that most of the audience had entered and seated themselves, they occupied just about every seat, certainly an encouraging bonus for the performers. The audience turned out as quite attentive and otherwise exceptional.

The urbane and friendly Modiano began the program by introducing himself and Beyond Baroque and advertising its purpose, its history, its foundation by George Drury Smith (from San Francisco), its bookstore, and so forth. After this opening Modiano graciously introduced Jack and Adelle Foley as our hosts; and from that point forward, appearing for all the world like a pair of poetic or troubadour vaudevillians, they took over the program. To judge from its commendable smoothness and ready pace, they had carefully prepared and organized the evening's entertainment. Most of the featured poets read well, handling the microphone with practised ease.

I recall from my own performing experience beginning in the late 1960s and early 1970s—when American poets overall started to read or recite poetry in public—how they proceeded rather tentatively, sometimes not assertively enough. By 2012 all that has changed: poets have become accustomed to reading aloud, and for the most part have emerged as real professionals at it. I can express only my gratitude and general admiration for this improvement, if not indeed genuine metamorphosis. Jack Foley introduced each poet in an apt and informed fashion, as the experienced master of ceremonies that he is. I cannot recall each poet and each poem read aloud, and so I shall content myself with some general observations, as well as detailed remarks where I can remember them.

As expected, I found it easier to grasp and recall the shorter pieces and those that seemed more formally arranged, even if not always cast in traditional forms per se. To *hear* a poem as read by its creator first, but before seeing the text, makes an unique experience, but without the text it becomes harder to recall after auditory assimilation. As the only African-American on the program, Will Alexander started the readings with a fairly long and rather surrealistic piece that I had trouble understanding, even if his sense of language and rhythm seemed competent and assured. At some point after Alexander, and probably some other poets (I forget the exact sequence), Adelle Foley read a highly structured sequence in her preferred medium—in this case, a series of highly structured haiku, vivid and evocative. Even if Adelle does not consider herself a formalist per se, the discipline apparent in her offering made a distinctive contrast to most of the poems by the other participants, largely in free verse and/or free form.

I should add here in an aside that by 7 December 2012, just before the Time-Line Night on the 8th, an L.A, City-organized committee including Dana Gioia elected the longtime poet and author Eloise Klein Healy, a genuine L.A. figure, as L.A.'s first poet laureate, whose work remains not only modern and substantial but also accessible and not obscure, formerly the bane of much modern poetry. This new position or office might as easily have gone to Wanda Coleman, a formidable poet, unable unfortunately to attend the Foleys' event at Beyond Baroque due to medical problems (also afflicting her husband Austin). Perhaps that will happen (I hope) on another occasion. The term of office runs for two years with an annual stipend of $10,000, which would form a treasure for most (impecunious) poets. As part of the job the poet laureate visits colleges and schools in a kind of outreach program, reading poetry and encouraging students in poetic and other scrivening vocations. As teacher and poet, E. K. Healy has already touched many lives and has already proven herself as an exceptional ambassador for poetry as well as writing in general.

Michael C. Ford presented one of the best poems of the evening, and in the liberated modern manner, an engaging and certainly moving tribute to another archetypal L.A. figure—and poet—James Douglas Morrison, otherwise Jim Morrison of The Doors, whom Ford addressed as a close friend with the affectionate name of "Jimbo" recurrent as a kind of refrain. J. D. M. had had several poetry collections published privately before his too early demise. It felt very good to have this reminder of the Hippie Days in L.A. and the San Francisco Bay Area.

As the doyen of the New Formalists (not their own term, but it has become affixed to the group), Dana Gioia preceded his poem with some choice and generous words à propos of Jack Foley's magnum opus. In addition, Gioia has written an excellent and abundant account (c. 600 words), an article-review, that will appear in *Poetry International,* which should greatly help expand Jack's audience. Gioia then read the beautiful elegy that he wrote in memory of his first son, who died after only four months. It was the first poem by Gioia that I read years agone, and it proved even more touching in his reciting of it from memory, its careful craftsmanship making it all the more indelible.

It was Jack Foley who first introduced me to the New Formalists by reading aloud a modern story in blank verse by David Mason, and letting me borrow his copy of Gioia's collection of essays on modern poetry, *Can Poetry Matter?* Later I bought a copy for my own library, no less than his second collection of essays, *Disappearing Ink.* These volumes rank as some of the best and most lucid appraisals of modern poets that I have encountered—warm, even-handed, and endlessly re-readable. Somewhere in this early lineup of poets reading at Beyond Baroque there appeared a tall and strapping young woman with long blond hair, who read quite effectively a long but cogent poem covering several pages. I cannot recall her name or her poem's ostensible subject, but I do remember its impressive impact on me. The poet in question is Kate Gale, as I now discover.

Many of these poets, in addition to those who followed, besides their status as L.A. poets, presented poems on L.A. subjects, a clearly logical choice, and generally they had cast them in free but disciplined verse. Many displayed a great sense of humor, sometimes hilarious, while they reflected on the vast ambiance covered by both L.A. city and county, as well as on the challenges and exigencies of living in L.A. as the original cityscape of endless freeways and endless housing tracts of remarkably similar dwellings and shopping malls. My own favorite of these L.A. poems remains the wry and funny piece by Suzanne Lummis, descended (as I discovered to my surprise and pleasure) from pioneering publisher Charles Lummis, whose house turned into a museum a while back somewhere in the eastern stretches of L.A. county. Charles made a point of featuring the work of Nora May French and Mary Austin in his magazines.

Much involved with the language and lore of the Amerindians

and/or the Hispanics living near or along what has turned into the U.S.-Mexican frontier, that is, residing on both sides—and commendably so—two poets from San Diego read next, and read well, and in one case, exceptionally. Having not encountered their work before (or at least as far as I can recall), I enjoyed meeting them and hearing them. However, I could not quite grasp and assimilate the several poems that each presented. Some seemed to be translations, and others appeared to be new poems based on translations. Rothenberg (well known and well regarded, as I apprehend) in particular offered as his final selection a poem in a language that I could not identify or understand, possibly in some Amerindian tongue, or if in English, put into sound by him in such a way (an unique type of highly repetitive singing or chanting, but based more on the speaking voice than on the regular singing one) that it baffled my comprehension, even as it also astonished. All in all, quite original!

Donald Sidney-Fryer, I myself, read next, first a choice extract from the criticism of S. T. Joshi, and then a short poem by me that Foley himself had chosen (as he did for everyone else), "An Enchantress out of Time," a particular favorite of Jack's. I declaimed it with as much fervor as I could muster, given the handicap of a microphone in such a limited hall, backing away so as not to explode the sound system. Even if what I read or recited took much less time and pages than that allowed to some of the other poets, I managed to make to my surprise some real kind of impact on the audience. After the overall program several people came up to congratulate me on the selection that I had read. One formalist had just finished, I myself, and another would follow him.

It thus became a genuine relief and pleasure to have one of the most notable of the New Formalists next at the podium, Timothy Steele. He preceded his own poem with some well-chosen (and for me, welcome) words concerning the beautiful experience of learning to express oneself in traditional forms, and also concerning the expansive possibilities inherent in those norms and forms, including the use of meter and rime. The poem that he quite articulately read aloud described a matutinal exchange (along a busy street near USC) between the poet as a "mere boy" of forty and a neighbor lady of eighty-two. He would give her a bouquet of his homegrown flowers, and in exchange she would give him some of her own homegrown lemons, the poem capturing perfectly a lovely, quiet, but meaningful moment between two friends.

Jack himself covered for the two featured poets who could not attend, David St. John and Paul Vangelisti, and read their selections for them. Amy Uyematsu presented her own distinctive offering in her own distinctive way. Ending the program, Jack and Adelle then read their own final selection together, the Hummingbird Chorus, sometimes one alternating with the other, and at other times joining their voices at the exact same time, but always clearly and with refreshing urgency. Their own readings, while often serious, are also a lot of fun.

While the two hosts were still standing at the podium, everyone else arose, and gave them a standing ovation, quite well deserved, both for their own offering and for arranging such an extraordinary program. It had become a true celebration of siblinghood, a feast of intellect and emotion. Many people stayed on, whether poet or spectator, congratulating and chatting with one another, and all with real warmth and amiability, despite all the differences in style, subject matter, and aesthetics. The evening represented a genuine triumph of culture and civilization. When John Miller drove himself and me back to my home, I could not help reflecting that I was, and am, jubilant that I had taken part. Thanks a lot, Jack and Adelle Foley, and thanks as well to Richard Mediano and Beyond Baroque. Warmest felicitations to them and all the participants!

As I close, I wish to express my deep gratitude for the emergence, two decades agone, of the New Formalists: not their own term, but now fixed in literary history. The best-known figures appear to be Dana Gioia, Timothy Steele, and David Mason. This all happened thanks to the controversy begun by the publication of an essay, twice under the same title, first in the *Atlantic Monthly* for April 1991, and then in a book issued in 1992 by Graywolf Press (St. Paul, Minnesota, 1992): *Can Poetry Matter?* by Dana Gioia. Due to this controversy, and then their consequent recognition, these poets have restored a much-needed and long-overdue balance to the ongoing evolution of American poetry and poetics. Emerging myself in 1961-71, I rejoice to have at last some valued company in my own formalist adventure!

Surrealism Is as Surrealism Does

Let us confront the aesthetic fact of life about surrealism at once, that is, about historical surrealism in art and literature. On the face of it, a good proportion of authentic surrealism appeared and still appears, at first consideration, so disorienting and illogical does it remain for many people, to be just so much nonsense—at best, enigmatic. That initial and admittedly superficial reaction becomes the first clue that it is absolutely not nonsense, even if we must always remember that all art is at least on one level *play,* albeit *serious* play.

Although surrealism as literature (above all in the form of poetry, as apart from polemical writing) first flourished from 1920 to 1925 under André Breton (1896-1966) as the French spokesman, surrealism overall, especially as associated with the painter Salvador Dalí (1904-1989), continued to flourish during the later 1920s and through the 1930s. During the mid-1940s it even went mainstream big time because of several major Hollywood feature films.

No one growing up in the 1930s and 1940s, especially in the U.S., could have ignored Dalí and surrealism. Being the consummate showman that he was, the canny Salvador well knew how to take advantage of any free publicity that came his way. The media everywhere, whether in Europe or the U.S., exploited him and his art to the maximum, simply because he always generated good copy, which the general public delighted to read. Here indeed existed an unique artist who lived up to the reputation of extravagance cultivated by artists past and present. There was a great deal to be said on behalf of that in a positive manner!

Nevertheless, other people with similar ideas and ideals, and one other prominent movement, flourished before surrealism came along. Thus authentic surrealism did have genuine predecessors. Like surrealism, the movement known as Dadaism, following World War I, featured accidental or incongruous effects in art and literature. Dadaism flowed easily and naturally into the greater surrealism. We should not fail to point out that the artists making up the Dadaist movement, like those making up the surrealistic movement, had all received a classical education, whether this involved Latin and Greek or the classical (traditional) art and literature of their own native land. In a sense, Dadaists and surrealists alike rebelled against the expectations fostered in them and in many other people by this classical education. They felt that the establishment with its customs and classical education had failed them, given the horrifying reality of World War I; and in one sense it had indeed failed them.

Perhaps, for our greater clarification, we should define, before we go any further, surrealism itself, borrowing aspects of our definition from various modern, accessible, and ubiquitous lexicons. We learn that surrealism is a style or movement in art and literature developed principally in the twentieth century, and that it emphasizes the subconscious (influenced here by the theories of Sigismund Freud and Pierre Janet) as well as the non-rational significance of imagery obtained by automatism or by exploitation of chance effects, or by unexpected (and apparently illogical) juxtapositions.

Whereas the adjective surrealistic can refer to the movement known as surrealism—at its greatest efflorescence during the 1920s (above all, during 1920-25)—the adjective surreal in popular use usually means that something has the disorienting, hallucinatory condition of a dream, and hence (by extension) the quality of something unreal or fantastic.

It is pertinent here to note that surrealism in painting means superrealism, but not (in one sense) photographic realism—rather a kind of magical realism that cannot manifest itself except by non-rational means (that is, non-ordinary or non-evidential means).

As already remarked, Breton and Dalí played the most important role as exemplars and promulgators of surrealism. Breton took it upon himself to become the active leader of the French surrealistic movement, the chief one. His poems, prose, and polemical writings on behalf of surrealism demonstrate his beliefs and his principles. His collaboration with fellow poet Philippe Soupault, *Les Champs Magnétiques* (*The Magnetic Fields*), first published in 1920, utilized what was to become the hallmark surrealist technique of automatic writing. His first Surrealist Manifesto appeared in 1924, defining surrealism as "psychic automatism in its pure state."

As a great Spanish painter, equal in value to Pablo Picasso, Dalí became the greatest surrealistic artist anywhere. Just as Breton officiated in France as the high priest of surrealism in literature and theory, so did Dalí as painter and illustrator function in Spain and in Europe at large as the high priest of surrealism in pictorial art. Dalí remains the greatest spokesman of surrealism—he was and still is Mr. Surrealism long after the chief efflorescence of the historical movement itself, and more than a quarter of a century following his death.

Nonetheless, odd as it may seem, Breton and Dalí with others do not by any means exhaust the full story of what we now call surrealism. In English, whether British or American, the entire corpus of literary surrealism hearkens all the way back to the halfway mark of the very long reign (1837-1901) of Queen Victoria. Surrealism in the literature of the English language begins with the so-called nonsense prose and poetry of Lewis Carroll (1832-1898), and also with the related humorous or nonsensical poetry of Edward Lear (1812-1888).

Literary historians generally describe Lewis Carroll, the English mathematician and writer, as having composed nonsense prose and poetry. They cite as outstanding examples *Alice's Adventures in Wonderland* (1865) and its sequel, *Through the Looking Glass* (1871). The latter includes "Jabberwocky" (also known as "The Ballad of the Jabberwock"), a supreme piece of the surrealistic imagination. We might also say the same for the slightly later narrative in verse, *The Hunting of the Snark* (1876). With Lewis Carroll we should probably bracket the wondrous Edward Lear, the perfectly respectable English landscape painter but utterly original nonsense poet—that is, the inspired writer of nonsense verse. However, as more than one ingenious and learned scholar has demonstrated (in some cases aided by the theories of Freud), nonsense poetry, whether by Carroll or Lear, often makes great good sense. (Oh, there was indeed a method to their madness!)

The continuing existence of surrealism in its modern development raises a legitimate problem of definition beyond what we have already attempted here. That is, what is the precise difference between Lewis Carroll's apparent nonsense on the one hand and the surrealism of André Breton and his coterie on the other hand? Or for that matter, what is the difference between certain types of surrealism and certain types of fantasy, whether of the modern period (the twentieth and twenty-first centuries) or of the Renaissance? In literature we are thinking in particular of the almost surrealistic imagery, constantly evolving or dissolving, as purveyed by Edmund Spenser (1552-1599) in his unique epic *The Faerie Queene* (1590, 1596, 1609), that immense cultural artifact that remains the perfect expression of the very long reign (1558-1603) of Elizabeth I. And in Italian painting of the same approximate period, in terms of the same surrealistic connections, we are thinking of the ingenious Giuseppe Arcimboldo (1527-1593), whose often bizarre canvases would have charmed the art connoisseurs of that age, as they have those of our own. Better known is the even earlier hallucinatory work of the Dutch painter Hieronymus Bosch (1450-1516).

Returning to the modern period, we should not overlook the two major motion pictures of the 1940s that have notable Dalí connections or Dalíesque affinities. First, *Lady in the Dark* (1944), starring the versatile Ginger Rogers, as directed and adapted by Mitchell Leisen from Moss Hart's innovative stage play, had metamorphosed into a slick Hollywood film, still rated highly for some rather original and surrealistic dream sequences very well and imaginatively presented, sequences that certainly deserve the adjective Dalíesque. Second, even more pertinently, we can cite Alfred Hitchcock's glossy Hollywood film *Spellbound* (1945), starring Ingrid Bergman and Gregory Peck. It has a memorable and magnificent dream sequence, aptly and spectacularly surrealistic, designed by Dalí himself. Greatly assisting the dreamlike mood of the film overall, the haunting main theme of Miklos Rozsa's music plays as strategic a role as that played by the two charismatic stars.

Even if the original (modern) surrealism, especially vis-à-vis the proto-surrealism of Lewis Carroll and Edward Lear during the extended Victorian period, took place during the 1920s, 1930s, and 1940s, it has definitely continued as an artistically durable and viable mode. Now during the first quarter of the twenty-first century it certainly comes vibrantly to life in the landmark volume that the reader presently holds in his or her hands.* It also serves as a perfect example of highly disciplined, echt-modern poetry—featuring and utilizing

---

*John Allen and Alan Gullette, *The Lighthouse Above the Graveyard: A Surrealist Séance* (CreateSpace, 2016).

to the nth degree the hallmarks of modern poetry—that is, free verse and free form. Indeed, this highly original dialogue between poets (and surrealist poets at that) furnishes the ultimate justification for the said free verse and free form. I am informed that they write in a vein that may be termed occult surrealism, in the sense that they both seek and deny a reality behind appearances. The least compliment that I can pay Messieurs John Allen and Alan Gullette is to recognize overtly that they have achieved something novel, innovative, and unprecedented in this substantial book in which they have combined their considerable talents.

To the Stars and Beyond

George Sterling. *Complete Poetry.* Edited by S. T. Joshi and David E. Schultz. Preface by Kevin Starr. New York: Hippocampus Press, 2013. 3 vols.

In opening our essay-review of George Sterling's complete collected poems (including his poetic dramas), we can do no better than to quote the first paragraph of the exceptional preface by the California historiographer Kevin Starr.

> This three-volume edition of the collected poetry of George Sterling, at once scrupulous in its editing and sumptuous in its presentation, represents a long overdue publishing tribute to an American poet who has received, almost simultaneously, too much attention and too little. At the core of the Sterling oeuvre, as presented in this volume, are evident the triumphs and dangers of regional reputation as well as the near obliteration of the late Romantic poets of the *fin-de-siècle* by literary critics of the mid- to late twentieth century.

This addresses at once the peculiar problems associated with Sterling and the California Romantics, including Clark Ashton Smith, who seems in his own case to have risen above them, especially the one of "datedness," of appearing outmoded or old-fashioned. In his useful and carefully calibrated book on Sterling brought out by Twayne in 1980, Thomas Benediktsson also points out the problem of datedness in Sterling's output.

> Clearly, Sterling did not understand the change in sensibility which generated Modernism; for better or for worse, he was of the *fin-de-siècle.* But in the 1920s [and also in the 1930s], fortunately for him, there were many poets and critics who shared his views. (131)

On the contrary, Sterling did indeed understand the Modernist change in sensibility; but neither he nor others with similar tastes much cared for it and its innovations, primarily on aesthetic grounds, never mind on intellectual ones. Fortunately for us, art and literature, unlike politics and religion, have infinite amplitude and variety. This explains the overall positive response to his last collections, whether during his lifetime or posthumously.

As Ashton Smith once expressed it, books are either well or poorly written: that is the bottom line, never mind the aesthetic or other theories supporting and informing them, even when their creators themselves do not always appear to be aware of them. Sterling's last collections include *Sails and Mirage* (1921), *Selected Poems* (1923), *Sonnets to Craig* (1928), *Poems to Vera* (1938), and *After Sunset* (1939). These books give strong emphasis to the fact that, after Sterling's death, his output did not vanish into the abyss of outer space.

Although Benediktsson's volume as a serious monograph remains almost unique in terms of critical attention focused on Sterling—it came forth in 1980, fifty-four years after his death and thrty-three years before the collected poems—yet Sterling's poetry, *mirabile dictu,* has continued to find publication and republication, even apart from the three magnificent volumes under consideration. As for the verdict of literary history in regard to the struggle (for supremacy?) between traditional and non-traditional poetry, the jury still is out and probably always will be, whether during the years between Sterling's death and the present or on into the future.

A word of caution: Starr and Benediktsson primarily discuss Sterling and his work in terms of American literature, sometimes also in terms of British and European (Continental) literature. The present reviewer will roam *ad libitum* across world literature (mostly European), from antiquity through the Middle Ages and the Renaissance on into the twenty-first century, and not just in English (American or British).

The set of the three volumes by Sterling follow in the wake of *The Complete Poetry and Translations of Clark Ashton Smith* (as also edited by Joshi and Schultz in three superb volumes, Hippocampus Press, New York, 2007–08) and *The Outer Gate: The Collected Poems of Nora Nay French* (as edited by Donald Sidney-Fryer and Alan Gullette, same publisher, 2009), all similar in format and mode of presentation: hardcover (the French volume is a trade paperback), 6 inches (width) by 9 (length) by 1 or 1½ (spine), with no cover art like that for the Smith poetry, whereas the total pagination for the Smith volumes runs around 1340 pp., that for the Sterling runs over 1300 pages, thus remarkably close in terms of quantity.

Although French's poetry will endure at best, alas, as no more than a slender volume (due to her early death in late 1907), both Sterling and Smith lived reasonably long and fulfilled lives as literary creators, and both achieved quite a sizeable corpus of work, above all in poetry. Sterling died in his latter fifties, Smith in his later sixties.

As usual (how fortunate that we can say that!) for Joshi and Schultz (and their many fine productions whether through Hippocampus or other publishers, whether anent editing and editorial matter), the three volumes by Sterling seem impeccable, very well researched, and beyond reproach; and possess the full appanage of preface, introduction, and notes. Each volume has the obligatory, but always useful, indices of titles and first lines, with divers appendices containing extra poems, selected appreciations, and a few surprises. Each volume has a different photo-portrait of Sterling, evidently taken toward the latter part of his life. The poet still appears noticeably handsome in all the photo-portraits.

A very nice touch: on the front cover of each volume appears the poet's signature stamped in gold, showing up against the dark blue of the cover's cloth, demonstrating again Sterling's lovely and regular penmanship. The reader would do well to read with extra care the excellent preface by Kevin Starr, who has long since revealed himself not only as an exceptional historian (whether general or specifically Californian), but also as a literary critic and historian of uncommon merit.

Volumes one and two more or less reproduce all Sterling's collections and poetic dramas. The latter became a special form of expression for Sterling. Some of the plays have made their début on the stage, where they function surprisingly well, unlike some poetic dramas by some of the Victorian poets, often marred by dramatic gaffes and other *bêtises*. Collecting the remainder of his poetry, volume three divides itself between "Dated Poems" and "Undated Poems"— and almost 500 pages ranks as the largest volume, featuring a variety of poems in divers forms and styles. Sterling reveals here and there quite a nice sense of humor, sometimes overt, and at other times rather sly, although in general he maintains a serious attitude as creator toward his own profession as poet, even if he sometimes made light of it when discussing it with other people.

For the record we list the contents of the three volumes. Volume 1,

Chords of Fire: The Testimony of the Suns, The Triumph of Bohemia (drama), *A Wine of Wizardry, The House of Orchids, Sonnets to Craig* (despite the name, a woman), *Poems to Vera, Beyond the Breakers, Yosemite: An Ode, The Caged Eagle, The Binding of the Beast* (some 60 poems inspired by World War I), and *Everyman* (drama).

Volume 2, *To a Girl Dancing: Lilith* (drama), *Rosamund* (drama), *Sails and Mirage* (this includes two of Sterling's best-known and best-loved poems "To a Girl Dancing" and "The Cool, Grey City of Love"), *Truth* (drama), *Truth: A Grove Play* (a second version adapted to the summer performance of plays at the Bohemian Grove north of San Francisco and an extension of the Bohemian Club in the City), *Strange Waters* (a pioneering but not uninteresting narrative about lesbians).

For those interested in Volume 3, entitled *The Stranger at the Gate,* please buy the volume, otherwise too copious and complicated for easy description. Although always competent and sometimes much more than that, in its traditional category, Sterling's poetry can still come up with the occasional surprise, humorous and otherwise.

As expected throughout this massive republication, pride of place goes to Sterling's often amazing sonnets. Little sequences of half a dozen poems or less clearly stand out, often augmented from one collection to another, sequences long since acknowledged and acclaimed: "Sonnets on Oblivion," "Sonnets on the Night Skies," "Sonnets on the Sea's Voice," "Sonnets by the Night Sea," "Omnia Exeunt in Mysterium," and "Ocean Sunsets." Overall, Sterling contributed to these sequences off and on from 1909 (*A Wine of Wizardry*) to 1921 (*Sails and Mirage*). Of course, the poet never contemplated publishing *Sonnets to Craig* and *Poems to Vera,* although they seem as competent and finished as any of the collections published in his lifetime.

Another point of comparison between Sterling and Smith: by our own rough count Sterling's total in these three volumes amounts to over 800 poems or separate items (including the poetic dramas or fragments of uncompleted ones), but his overall total probably amounted to over 1000 pieces. Smith's total in his three volumes easily surpasses 1000 items. Sterling's poetic dramas (or fragments thereof) probably amount to 300 pp. or more and bulk large in his overall output, occupying the same place but not as large, obviously, as Ashton Smith's fiction does in the latter's oeuvre.

We should preface our discussion of Sterling's life and works with a few remarks on the general state of poetry current in the American part of the English-speaking world, if not indeed in other parts of the world overall, in other languages and literatures. Thanks first to the British Empire and now to the British Commonwealth, as well as to the prominence if not the preeminence of the U.S. since World War II, English has willy-nilly become the universal tongue of our human-dominated planet, however unsuitable in a variety of aspects.

Spanish would easily make a better choice in terms of grammar, syntax, accentuation, spelling, etc., than English with its linguistic heritage divided primarily between Anglo-Saxon and Norman French, not to mention Greek, Latin, and the Latin-derived languages. As it is, Spanish must rank close after English in terms of people speaking it internationally. An enormous number of people speak the languages and dialects of Russia, China, and India. That is undeniable, but these language-users are mostly confined to the landmasses of those countries.

It follows then that, willy-nilly, many non-native English-speaking people have come to know and study in depth the historic panorama of English language and literature with all their bizarre and peculiar idiosyncrasies, from Old English, Medieval, Early Modern, and Modern, whether or not they deserve that prominence or preeminence. We speak here of things linguistical as they exist today, and not as they might have turned out otherwise, even if such speculation seems natural and often amusing.

When he died in his early seventies, Walt Whitman (1819-1892) must have taken some satisfaction in the fact that he had effected a wide-ranging and profound change, an innovation in one of the most significant arts, not only that of literature but more specifically that of poetry, generally more loved and esteemed outside the U.S. This innovation led to free verse and free form, a radical but useful extension of prosody from strictly metrical to a more flexible (non-metrical) approach. This involved, of course, a novel and more "natural" approach to poetic rhythm, rather than that of fulfilling older metrical schemes, so that poetry could have a richer and more nuanced freedom of rhythm like that of prose. The term *vers libre* came into French in 1902, and then that of its English equivalent, *free verse* (into American and British English) in 1908. As a medium, free verse remains close to the poem in prose, as first developed in France, and largely by Aloysius Bertrand, Baudelaire, and Rimbaud. Nonetheless, free verse and the prose-poem remain two distinct means of literary expression.

Let us discuss a little this new non-metrical approach, as evidenced in that revolutionary, echt-American volume *Leaves of Grass* (first published in 1855, and then in its final edition in 1891-92). Incidentally, the shorter poems generally work better than the longer ones, especially the rhapsodical catalogues. The short opening poem "Out of the cradle endlessly rocking" remains an unusually distinctive piece. Each line is memorably varied and exceptionally incisive, especially for free verse, and here we come to the crux of the matter via-à-vis traditional poetry.

The latter as its best really does make the metrical scheme emphasize the statement or subject matter, and in a way stronger than what free verse and/or free form usually achieve, by the nature of the words embedded in the metrical scheme with or without rime. (Rime at best makes the incisiveness even more pronounced.) Because many poets at first perceived Walt Whitman's innovation as making the composition or creation of poetry too facile, they tended to disdain it as somehow illegitimate. But gradually, as more and more people used it, it gained acceptance and respect. However, the differences between traditional and non-traditional remain profound, if not divisive.

Opening up this new means of poetic realization represents a major step forward, whereby many people since the late nineteenth and early twentieth centuries have found a mode of poetic expression congenial to them. If at one time strict form and meter enabled people to discover the poetry that they were seeking out of themselves (say, Chaucer and then Spenser, as well as the other great poets in England and elsewhere in Europe), many people, chafing under the restrictions imposed by traditional form and meter, sought a poetic mode that gave them greater freedom to say what they wanted to say. They found this freedom in Whitman's remarkable innovation, and not just in English but in many other languages.

Since his time, but more particularly since Eliot and Pound in the 1920s, more and more poets (more than a few ranking as great figures) have taken up and often excelled in this new mode or medium. For convenience we can use the terms traditional or non-traditional to designate poets and poetry all inclusively. The new, non-traditional poetry did not find at first a warm welcome, but gradually poets and critics accepted it, and it is now the reigning mode. However, following their own convictions, many poets have continued to write in traditional form or forms. Much of their best work often ranks in value next to the best work done by their predecessors. All good or great poetry demands considerable talent, practice, and labor. "Each verse means work, and none comes free," whatever the form or medium chosen. In a way free verse or free form is a misnomer.

Quite apart from the people who relished this new medium (that is, of non-traditional poetic expression), this innovation or revolution—more or less complete sometime between the 1920s and 1950s—left many traditional poets high and dry, stranded now somewhere between grudging acceptance and scorn or disdain for their apparent lack of novelty and enterprise. Some of these poets of an increasingly abandoned style of expression happen to rank as unequivocally great figures, even if not as well known as their admirers would like. George Sterling and Ashton Smith, at least in the U.S. (they do have their admirers abroad), remain prime examples of great poetic figures caught somewhere between two presumably contrary forces or conditions, the one traditional, the other non-traditional. Ashton Smith's popularity because of his prose fictions has forced attention back onto his poetry and then that of his great mentor, as well as others of the California Romantics.

Thus, what might have become a greater general recognition for this group across the U.S. and even into the then British Empire—Sterling already had achieved some of this, but not Ashton Smith as his protégé—became instead, to speak metaphorically, a fading or abandoned religion, with the former devotees flocking to the altars of these exciting new gods and their own particular cult, a cult that seemed to promise much more than it would be able to deliver. Thus denied this greater fame and recognition, whether before or after Sterling's death in late 1926, Ashton Smith eventually turned to writing prose fantasies of extraordinary linguistic distinction for *Weird Tales, Wonder Stories,* and other pulp magazines of the 1920s and 1930s, whereas in the main the 1940s witnessed the extinction of such periodicals.

What then of George Sterling, his poetry and career, in the meanwhile? He had enjoyed that rare fortunate life that can happen on occasion. Born in 1869 in the former whaling port of Sag Harbor, New York, Sterling went west in 1890 and went to work as a clerk for his uncle, Frank C. Havens, who had gone west earlier and had since become a real-estate magnate in Oakland. Sterling first lived with his relatives but eventually moved to San Francisco while continuing to work for his uncle, taking the ferry back and forth. He worked for him until 1905, when his aunt gave him his "freedom money" (so called), wherewith he moved from the City and bought land in Carmel. There he proceeded to build one or more houses or cabins, and there he invited his fellow Bohemians in the City to come down and settle in that lovely region. It was he who made Carmel into an art colony.

Sterling had already met several well-known literary figures, Joaquin Miller, Ambrose Bierce, and Jack London, who became his close friends. Although he had written some poetry in his youth and early adulthood, Sterling began writing poetry seriously around the mid-1890s, uniquely under the tutelage of Bierce. Dedicated to his poetic master, his first collection, *The Testimony of the Suns,* appeared in 1903, and his last major one, the *Selected Poems,* in 1923. Although strikingly different, Sterling as a poet probably stands next to someone like Longfellow. To rank Sterling next to Longfellow represents not just a compliment but something approaching the truth. We do not intend in this account to follow Sterling's life and career in detail, but we must at least state that Sterling became known as the great poet that he remains (mass popularity need not apply here) but also as a Bohemian, man about town, musician, historian, critic, and columnist (for the *Overland Monthly*). Within its limits, Sterling's poetry is genuine and solid, as well as enlightening.

Compared to so much of the formless and often insipid poetry of today (too often, trivially autobiographical), how refreshing Sterling's poetry appears in retrospect with its extraordinary tone and music, its élan and panache, its unfashionable poetic attitudinizing, its unfettered but stylistically apt vocabulary, its often unconventional subject matter and cosmic philosophy, even if rather unfriendly to the human species! Where does a reader or critic begin to do justice to such a lavish feast of imagery, sound, and sentiment? While continuing in the great Romantic tradition of Shelley, Keats, Coleridge, and Wordsworth, Sterling expands that inheritance, its depth and range, to include not just things immediately relevant to planet Earth and species *Homo sapiens.* That he like Ashton Smith often comes up with a negative assessment works to our advantage. Thanks to Sterling, we become free of provincialism, cosmic or human; and the imagination like a jet airplane or spacecraft can take off toward unknown stars and shores. Such a poetic art and vision, like Smith's, are unique.

Let us quote some typical samples of Sterling's exceptional stanzas and lines. The problem here is that so much of it is highly quotable and impressive. We shall start at the beginning with his first collection (*The Testimony of the Suns*) and end with the last original one (*Sails and Mirage*).

From the title poem of *The Testimony of the Suns* one may quote at random and come up with something well worth pondering:

> O armies of eternal night,
> > How flame your guidons on the dark!
> > Silent we turn from Time to hark
> What final Orders sway your might.
>
> What music from Capella runs?
> > How hold the Pleiades their bond?
> > How storms the hidden war beyond
> Orion's dreadful sword of suns?
>
> How haste the unresting feet of Change,
> > On life's stupendous orbit set!
> > She walks a way her blood hath wet,
> Yet thinks her path untrodden, strange.

From the title poem of *A Wine of Wizardry* one may similarly quote at random and find such wonderful sententious lines:

> So Fancy's carvel seeks an isle afar,
> Led by the Scorpion's rubescent star,
> Until in templed zones she smiles to see
> Black incense glow, and scarlet-bellied snakes
>
> Sway to the tawny flutes of sorcery.
> There priestesses in purple robes hold each
> A sultry garnet to the sea-linkt sun,
> Or, just before the colored morning shakes
> A splendor on the ruby-sanded beach,
> Cry unto Betelgeuse a mystic word.

From *The House of Orchids,* probably his single best collection before the *Selected Poems* of 1923, one may again quote at random, as exemplified in this piece, number II from "Sonnets on the Sea's Voice":

> No cloud is on the horizon, and on the sea
>   No sail: the immortal, solemn ocean lies
>   Unbroken sapphire to the walling skies—
> Immutable, supreme in majesty.
> The billows, where the charging foam leaps free,
>   Burden the winds with thunder. Soul, arise!
>   For ghostly trumpet-blasts and battle-cries
> Across the tumult wake the Past for thee.
>
> They call me to a dim, disastrous land,
>   Where fallen marbles tell of mighty years,
>   Heroic architraves, but where the gust
> Ripples forsaken waters. Lo! I stand
>   With armies round about, and in mine ears
>   The roar of harps reborn from legend's dust.

We pass by with little comment the *Sonnets to Craig* and the *Poems to Vera,* even if they have in abundance some excellent examples no less quotable. All the poems of both sequences well reward careful reading. From *Beyond the Breakers* we quote Sterling's literally ineffable sonnet in tribute to "The Muse of the Incommunicable":

An echo often have our singers caught,
    And they that bend above the saddened strings;
    One hue of all the hundred on her wings
Our painters render, and our men of thought
In realms mysterious her face have sought
    And glimpsed its marvel in elusive thin s.
    Her fragrance gathers and her shadow clings
To all the loveliness that man hath wrought.

The wind of lonely places is her wine.
    Still she eludes us, hidden, husht, and fleet;
    A star withdrawn, a music in the gloom.
Beauty and death her speechless lips assign,
    Where silence is, and where the surf-loud feet
        Of armies wander on the sands of doom.

From *The Caged Eagle* we cite an apt sample of Sterling mixing past and present in a bit of praise "To the Hummy of the Lady Isis" (underneath the title: IN THE BOHEMIAN CLUB, SAN FRANCISCO):

No bird shall tell thee of the season's flight:
    Sealed are thine ears that now no longer list.
    The little veins of temple and of wrist
Are food no more for sleepless love's delight,
And crumbling in the sessions of thy night,
    Pylon and sphinx shall be as fleeting mist.
    Bitter with natron are the lips that kissed,
And shorn of dreams the spirit and the sight.

Ah! dust misused! better to feed the flower,
Than grace the revels of an alien hour,
    When babe or lord wake never to caress
        The bosom where unerring Death hath struck
        And milkless breasts that gave the ages suck—
    Stilled in the slumber that is nothingness.

While not generally well regarded, the poems in *The Binding of the Beast* (mostly sonnets) are technically excellent and not without a certain bizarre (if unintended) humor given the subject matter. "The Crown Prince at Verdun" is a good example of Sterling's ready versatility:

> By Mars his hilt! this is a royal sport,
>   And fit amusement for a king-to-be!
>   Surely the revels now permitted thee
> Excel the poor diversions of a court!
> Against the tireless thunder of the fort
>   Thy ranks go forth as waves upon a sea
>   Puppets and pawns that move at thy decree.
> A merry game, but mayst thou find it short!
>
> Or is it as a painter that thy skill
>   Favors the world?—daubing with red the snow,
> As on the mighty canvas oaf hill
>   Thy cannon spread the pigments, till the whole
>   Stands perfect, and applauding armies know
>   The vision of the Hell that waits thy soul.

From *Sails and Mirage* we cite as our final sample another superb sonnet "The Wine of Illusion," once more dealing with misperception—or is it imagination?—without which our species could not function:

> I saw One clad in opalescent grey;
>   Who held a crystal cup within her hands
>   In which a sun was deathless. Mighty wands
> Shook as the spears of starlight in each ray,
> And where they smote, the darkness was as day,
>   And where they smote not, night was on the lands.
>   Beneath her feet dead stars were strewn like sands,
> And in her wings the constellations lay.
>
> "Of this have all men drunken deep," she said.
>   "Drink this or perish. There is naught beside.
>   This is the draught that fashions men from swine,
>   And though thy heart deny me in its pride,
> Yet of my cup of dreams its blood is red
>   And thy lips red with my creative wine!"

Even if we do not quote anything from them, Sterling's poetic dramas are also full of endlessly quotable lines, whether in the dialogue or in the songs dispersed throughout them. We recommend that the reader explore them with care in order to discover the myriad beauties that constitute their essence.

In a very real and multifaceted sense we may doubt that Ashton Smith would have developed into the poet that he became without Sterling and his pioneer cosmic poetry. Smith took what he got from Sterling; and adding to what inhered within himself (his own self-education in literature and poetry among much else) and from his local environment and cosmic ambiance, he developed it further, deepened and heightened it. As we have defined it elsewhere (the front flap of the dust jacket for Smith's own *Selected Poems*, 1971):

> Inspired by the example of his poetic mentor George Sterling and his two greatest poems *The Testimony of the Suns* (1903) and *A Wine of Wizardry* (1907),—long before the early science fiction and fantasy magazines,—Clark Ashton Smith was creating an unique type of fantasy and science fiction in verse whose metaphysical and psychological depths have yet to be discovered, charted, and explored [by the literary mainstream].

However, this definition applies just as well to Sterling's own poetry, although Sterling usually lacks Smith's cosmic "ruthlessness" or "indifference." In his pursuit of what he regarded as the truth, Smith like Bierce takes no prisoners—that is, he does not compromise. Not that Sterling is a bleeding heart: far from it. Overtly his poetry here and there shows a more obvious humanity. Nonetheless, if his detailed and long-term encouragement of Ashton Smith (as revealed in the letters between them during 1911-26) will always reflect great credit and honor on the elder poet, so shall Smith's own work, but even more, accomplish the same for Sterling as his own poet and person.

In a sense George Sterling, Ashton Smith, and Nora May French, along with others (we might include Bierce both as poet and Sterling's poetic mentor), represent California's "classical poets," more especially in their traditionalism, impeccable craftsmanship, and outward-reaching cosmicism, even if individually or collectively they still remain comparatively unknown to the mainstream (Californian or U.S.), literary and otherwise. As Ashton Smith himself becomes better known, he will probably carry the California Romantics with him into the future, thus repaying the debt to Sterling and others.

How many poets have their complete collected poems published or republished, particularly when they thus remain relatively unknown to the literary and artistic mainstream of the later twentieth and early twenty-first centuries? Unless very well known, such complete republication is rare indeed. Without Derrick Hussey (as an enlightened publisher with a wide knowledge and appreciation of literature and poetry past and present), S. T. Joshi, and David E. Schultz, this collective republication of Sterling's entire poetic output (as extant in libraries) would probably never have happened.

As in the case of the complete collected poetry of Ashton Smith, the similar publication (in three large volumes) of Sterling's complete poetic oeuvre represents a staggering and long-term amount of sheer labor, whether involving original research (mostly in libraries public or university), conscientious copying, or textual comparison and preparation—even with computers, the Internet, and so forth. All honor to Messieurs Joshi and Schultz, not to mention the brave and enterprising publisher!

If Arkham House as a specialist publishing firm under August Derleth proved unique during the 1940s, 1950s, and 1960s, up through 1971, because it published some highly imaginative poetry (usually fantastic and/or macabre)—two anthologies, and volumes by Leah Bodine Drake, Donald Wandrei, Ashton Smith, and Donald Sidney-Fryer (this last-named poet just made it under the wire before Derleth's death in mid-1971)—then Hippocampus Press has far surpassed Arkham House itself in this one genre. May all possible kudos go to the triumvirate of Hussey, Joshi, and Schultz!

A Journey Beyond All Journeys

A REPORT ON NECRONOMICON III

An account of a trip from Sacramento (Woodland), California, to Providence, Rhode Island, to Sandwich, Cape Cod, Massachusetts, to Portland (Bridgton), Maine, and then back to Cape Cod, Providence, and Sacramento: from Wednesday, 16 August through 31 August 2017.

How did it happen that I, Donald Sidney-Fryer, attended the Lovecraft convention at Providence, Rhode Island, the NecronomiCon III, 17–20 August 2017? Because the people behind the Con make a point of having a poet laureate during the Con's duration—in accordance with the civilized literary standards associated with fictioneer, poet, essayist, and epistolarian H. P. Lovecraft (1890–1937)—my chief publisher Derrick Hussey, the owner-editor of Hippocampus Press (New York), proposed my name to the chairman, Niels (-Viggo) Hobbs, for the role or position of the current event. Niels accepted the proposal. Thus I became not just one of the Guests of Honor but according to the official literature a Special Guest of Honor, thus a double recognition, as properly registered by myself, as honoree, and with gratitude.

Derrick and Niels both set this up much earlier in 2017, which year's number may possess a clandestine numerological significance. Do I credit numerology in and of itself? Well, I don't disbelieve. I find it suggestive, and certainly aesthetic, especially the seven, one of the prime numbers, if memory serves. At least a good omen or augury, in the style of the Greeks and Romans. Of course, I accepted the honor, even if I have ceased to find conventions exciting or of real interest. I accepted with enthusiasm, which gradually declined or lay dormant or quiescent in the intervening months before the great event. This was how I thought or felt, or how I had reached a nominal conclusion.

In the last few years, since I turned eighty-one (on 8 September 2015), but even more so since I turned eighty-two (2016), instead of feeling confident and special in a variety of ways, I have become plagued by self-doubt—nothing really bad, but annoying and awkward, even if not impeding me in any manner. Also during the last year or so I've become disenamored of traveling. I like sojourning for a while in a different locale, but going there and coming back by airplane, passing through customs or security with close inspection, leaves me less than charmed, however needed for safety and other concerns. Safety *is* essential.

The closer we approached the Con in time, I began to feel reluctant, instead of excited, however signal the honor to me as one of the selected guests, all expenses paid more or less. But dear, kind, and generous Derrick had already gone to much trouble for me, and I had no intention of not honoring my acceptance of functioning as poet laureate. Besides, I enjoy performing poetry in a manner clear, clean, and strong—that is, with nuance and vividness. Derrick duly sent me the paper copies of my e-tickets, duly downloaded, plus other connected material.

Dear Don Lynch, who lives in the main house next to where I reside, in my garage changed into a charming cottage, agreed to take me to the Sacramento Airport (15 or 20 minutes away by car) on 16 August, Wednesday morning for my flight at 10:40, although we left the house around 8:30, to allow for the preliminary time before takeoff. Later he would pick me up on my return back from the Northeast on 31 August, Thursday evening. Meanwhile I finished up various writing projects, happy to take a vacation from the eternal proofing, editing, and the usual small amount of rewriting.

Derrick had benevolently published what might remain my very last book, *Aesthetics Ho! Essays on Art, Literature, and Theatre,* which concludes with what is indeed my last collection of poetry, *Ends and Odds,* thus balancing out my previous volume, my autobiography *Hobgoblin Apollo,* which concludes with my previous collection of poetry, *Odds and Ends* (1916). At my request Derrick timed my latest book's appearance to coincide with the NecronomiCon in Providence. For this last volume I had created two tributes, one in prose, one in verse: "H. P. Lovecraft—A Belated Homage" and "To H. P. L.—A Tribute out of Time."

I should add that, while these two books will probably remain my two very last ones intentionally created, I still have my magnum opus, *The Case of the Light Fantastic Toe,* to publish in some form or fashion. This is an enormous monograph on the European ballet theatre from c. 1820 up to 1921, highlighting the Romantic Ballet begun in 1831 or 1832 and finishing sometime very early in the 1900s. A trial edition published by Lulu, 6 × 9 inches, 40 lines of easily readable text, totals some 3000 printed pages. It took me about twenty years to compose and compile. The research began in the 1950s and continued off and on until I began the composition in 1980, as well as during the actual writing. From November 2015 through September 2017, thanks to the scanning of the typescript by Alan Gullette, I have proofed and reproofed the overall text some four times, thus making about two extra years to prepare the text for publication of any type. What sparked my interest in the subject? The ballet theatre of the nineteenth century features a strong fantastic element.

After finishing up my more or less last project, or part of a project, the big, long-awaited leave-taking for the Con took place. On Tuesday I had packed my non-rigid overnight bag with essential changes of clothing, no less than my shoulder bag, the latter with toiletries and pills, even more essential, thus arranged for instant access. Don brought me to the airport by 8:45 A.M. and dropped me off, with plenty of time for the flight and the preliminary business.

Traveling on American Airlines or affiliates, we arrived in Providence an hour later than scheduled, 11:00 P.M. instead of 10:00 P.M., due to the lateness of the connecting flight out of Chicago. Otherwise it turned out a routine flight; the plane did not crash, and I had no colonic accident. On both planes I managed to get an aisle seat, ideal to avoid a colonic mishap, instant access to any restroom. The people behind the Con had not been able to arrange the aisle seats for me.

No one from the Con, or the hotel where I would stay (the Providence Biltmore), met me at the airport, nor did I see the shuttle buses going to the hotels, beyond where people were picking up friends and relatives, fellow passengers who had landed with me in Rhode Island. I went up to a very pleasant middle-aged lady, on the scene to pick up her daughter, and asked if she perchance hailed from the Con. She did not so hail, and I explained my dilemma.

When her college-aged daughter showed up (I had moved back with my bags to my seat under the protective roof), they embraced and conferred with each other. The daughter came over to offer me a ride to the hotel; where they were going themselves was not far away. Rather tired after getting up at 5:30 that morning, I eagerly accepted their life-saving offer. After 15 or 20 minutes we arrived at the hotel in downtown Providence, I thanked them very warmly, and they drove off.

Entering the luxurious lobby, I went up to the night clerk on duty at the main counter. I told him my name and explained that I had come for the Lovecraft Con; he gave me an envelope from Niels Hobbs with my name on it, welcoming me to the event. It contained the program of the events in which I was to participate. He also gave me one of those electronic keys to my suite, Room 1234, quite a luxurious ambiance as it developed.

I hoisted my bags up once more and soon found myself at last in my temporary abode for five nights and four full days, Thursday, Friday, Saturday, and Sunday. Laying down my bags, I found myself alone at last, free from other people. After laying out some of my gear here and there, especially my toiletries in part of the bathroom, the counter with the wash basin, I took a quick shower, dried off, and went under the duvet on one of the twin king-sized beds and promptly fell asleep. I woke up before 8 A.M., dressed, and went down to eat my breakfast in the fine restaurant maintained in the hotel.

Then I returned to the peace and quiet of my suite, to study my part in the convention's program. Niels had arranged a full schedule for me, but generally with enough space between events so I could take a break in the bar off the dining room or rest in my private chambers. The chairman of the Con, along with the others forming the convention committee, had arranged the four-day affair at two fancy hotels only a block or so from each other, within easy access: the Providence Biltmore Hilton and the Omni Hotel (pronounced OM-nee: I believe there was or is a science fiction magazine of that name), both high-rises but not skyscrapers. I would estimate that some 2000 people may have attended the Con, and the vendor rooms were located on the first and second floors of the Omni. Whenever I checked on them, they seemed full of customer-attendees eagerly buying books and other memorabilia. My own chief publisher Hippocampus Press appeared to be doing quite well with sales, including my own titles. Literary quality aside, the books must sell so that the publisher can remain in business and publish further deserving authors and volumes.

I did not get to meet the owner-editor until the opening ceremony at the First Baptist Church (in America), in the upper and grander of the two main auditoriums contained therein. The ceremony thus took place in this very large historic space, Barnaby Evans acting as emcee and opening the program. Steven J. Mariconda followed with a fine and finely delivered account of Lovecraft's life and career, and then a local woman, an excellent historian, recounted some of Rhode Island's historical firsts achieved as a colony and then as a state, mentioning the often close connections between these events and those in Lovecraft's fiction and poetry. However, this estimable lady demonstrated very few of these connections beyond simply mentioning them—that is, hardly at all, alas! On their own these revelations of Rhode Island's past as colony and state proved rather amazing.

Summoned to come forth at the very last, I presented three short but appropriate sonnets of my own, ending with the recently factured "To Howard Philips Lovecraft—A Tribute out of Time," which features pointed and suggestive references to his cosmic-astronomic-mindedness, to his fabled and fictitious tome, the *Necronomicon,* to several tales major and minor, as well as to his Ancient Ones. Like everyone else featured on the program, I used the handy microphone, marvelous invention indeed. For me the highlight became the "perfect musical accompaniment" (per the program literature) as provided by the indeed "internationally renowned organist" Gigi Mitchell-Velasco, a trained operatic soprano as well. In fact, until someone explained it to me, I had thought that two performers presided at the organ, the organist and the singer. I had wanted to confer with Gigi, not only to talk with her about her superb performance, but the modern and inherited repertoire of organ music, not just J. S. Bach and Max Reger but Franz Schmidt. His organ works remain large-scale symphonic morceaux of enduring fascination and supreme value, if not in fact the culmination of the First Vienna School from Haydn and Mozart through Brahms, Bruckner, and Mahler, but all founded on the "magical" and abundant organ works of J. S. Bach. Gigi finished her "accompaniment" with a brief but very cute version of "Yes! We Have No Bananas," followed by the Prelude and Fugue in C Minor of J. S. Bach. This piece reminded me that his organ works after all remain music for performance in church or temple. After Gigi finished, I had hoped to compliment her on her playing, to discuss aspects of the organ repertoire, but I could not find her after the program.

I shall give as compact an account as I can of the Con per se, but mostly of my part in it, as arranged by Niels Hobbs. Friday, Saturday, and Sunday went by so fast, as I ran from one place to the other, that in memory it now seems no more than a, fast-moving kaleidoscope. Zip goes the film!

On Friday, 18 August, mid-morning, I served on a panel discussing that singular author Ambrose Bierce, who influenced so positively George Sterling and Ashton Smith. In the early afternoon I appeared on a panel discussing the latter poet and fictioneer, a highly gratifying experience. Finally during the late afternoon all nine or ten guests of honor made their appearance and introduction on a panel, superlatively moderated by s. j. bagley [*sic*]. He ran in front of the table with the panelists from one to the other, an amazing demonstration of intellectual, emotional, and psychic power. Friday terminated with the Eldritch Ball (masquerade) from mid-evening to midnight or so. I did not attend but went to bed early instead.

Saturday for me went by no less rapidly. I appeared on a panel anent Arthur Machen in the early afternoon. Thanks to Lovecraft and his great admiration for Machen (shared by Ashton Smith), the Welsh author occupies today an universally respected and acknowledged position in the weird fiction genre. Then came two panels on weird poetry, the first in the late afternoon, ably and sensitively augmented by Frank Coffman, the professor and specialist on the copious poetry by Robert E. Howard. The real revelation here was the brilliant classical Greek scholar Sonya Taaffe as the adroit moderator, when at my humble request she recited the opening lines of the *Odyssey* in classical Greek. What an apocalypse!

The final poetry panel, scheduled as a workshop, proved even more apocalyptic than the first thanks to the younger poets who held forth, or as in the case of Stanley Gemmell, an established and authoritative poet of unusual strength but apparently without a published collection. He should have served as the elder poet present, not myself. Stanley read with an unbelievable intensity a kind of love poem, celebrating some actual or ideal female beauty of the human species. Stanley projects poetry in the manner in which it should be: dynamic, clear, clean, with nuance and subtle humor: the ideal of serious play that constitutes poetry on the highest level. His recitation or reading utterly knocked me down, knocked me over—unprecedented and overwhelming!

On Sunday morning I woke up too late to attend the "Cthulhu Prayer Breakfast," which is, without entering into the matter conspicuously, anathema to me. Nobody had scheduled anything for me on Sunday, a panel or what-have-you (for which I give thanks). Although I had wanted to attend a panel on William Hope Hodgson in the early afternoon, I stayed instead in my room and attended to personal needs that the programming so far had not allowed me to do. Washing my hair, shaving, washing a few garments by hand, trimming my hair, beard, and moustache (those durn unruly wire-like hairs that obstinately stick out). Then I exercised, subsequently taking a nap. Once awake, I dressed and circulated, and joined a late-afternoon group in the hotel bar with Derrick and others for drinks and food. Thus the day completed itself.

Apart from Gigi's excellent organ performance on Thursday, one other thing happened that meant as much to me, perhaps even more. Getting to know the remarkable poet (and no less personable individual) Stanley Gemmell became on Saturday afternoon the Con's highlight for me. He had brought with him a whole pile of my own books (authored or edited) for me to sign for, or to, him, always a highly flattering ritual for any author, particularly one as esoteric as myself. We were sitting outside the capacious room where the Arthur Machen panel discussion would occur.

During our exchange various other aficionados came up to me and also had me sign copies of my books, some of them recently purchased in one of the vendor rooms. Even the pleasant young man on duty as a "Minion" outside the door to the Machen panel went and bought a copy of *The Atlantis Fragments* (in its trade paperback edition) for me to sign! All this proved quite gratifying, to say the least. I have so few genuine admirers of my literary arts that I cherish any and all of them as long-lost family, if not children, given my age at eighty-three.

On Friday evening something else happened, just as extraordinary and meaningful. My nephew Jim with his older daughter Angelina drove all the way from Manhattan to Providence to visit with me, at the same time as Jim's younger daughter Lorraine drove down from Boston to do likewise. In Jim and Angelina's case that represents about 200 miles, and in Lorraine's case about 40 or 50 miles. Although I was a little late getting down to the hotel lobby from my room to meet and greet them, meet we did. We spent several wonderful hours together in a booth in the hotel restaurant, eating dinner, conversing, and having a marvelous time of it. I can't thank Jim and his daughters sufficiently for literally going to such extraordinary lengths just to see me, and so we could all have an unprecedented visit collectively. They are not only close relatives but great friends. I remain flabbergasted!

On Sunday evening, after parting from Derrick and company, I returned to my room, but not before I had a long and significant exchange with Christopher Geissler, the Director of Special Collections in the John Hay Library at Brown University in Providence. Librarians in general remain my favorite people, if not culture heroes; very well informed and often impassioned, but in an understated manner. Christopher proved no exception, and we discussed the manifold riches of the Lovecraft Collection, which also includes abundant papers, letters, and manuscripts of stories by Ashton Smith, as safeguarded and then donated by Lovecraft's nephew R. H. Barlow. Cosmic blessings on Bob Barlow for preserving such and so much precious material!

During the latter morning of Monday, 21 August 2017, by prearrangement, my cousin Gail's husband Paul Scannell drove over from their home in East Sandwich, northwest Cape Cod, and came to pick me up while I was at the Providence Biltmore. At that point the most rewarding and extended part of my sojourn back east began. I had arranged my flight back to Sacramento so that I could spend special time with Gail and Paul, and also with Ron, Fran, and Glenn (brother, sister-in-law, and their eldest son) not quite 50 miles northwest of Portland, Maine. I had not visited any close relatives in the Northeast for quite a few years, and the NecronomiCon III provided the perfect means. Benedictions on Derrick H. and Niels Hobbs.

However, being personal, the account of staying overnight with Gail and Paul, and then with the family in Maine, I can tell in a much smaller compass. I first planned to spend the longer part of my sojourn with Gail and Paul, and then the shorter part in Maine before flying back home. Gail and Paul wisely reversed this order, and so I'm passing the last and longer part with the latter. No kinder and more attractive hosts could exist! And they should encounter no problem driving me back to the Providence Airport, about an hour or more away by car, from their home in East Sandwich.

As I find myself in the midst of the family sojourn right now, I cannot help but reflect how differently these two weeks (or a little less), 16–31 August 2017, are turning out as compared with the less than two months that I spent in El Salvador with Jesse Allen and his assistant Eric Marenco. Not only did that earlier period, late November 2016 through late January 2017, make me feel anxiety, disappointment, betrayal, but above all anger and even rage.

My closest friends know the story, and I need not, and will not, badmouth Jesse and Eric, but unless they return to me some of that which they exacted from me, I shall find myself gravely compromised in a year or so—that is, in terms of keeping myself alive, independent, and in relative comfort. No greater contrast could exist between my last El Salvador adventure and my current New England sojourn.

After arriving at Paul and Gail's enchanting Cape Cod abode, I soon settled in. Their home stands in the midst of not quite a full acre in an ambiance of trees, bushes, and lavish natural beauty. A former attached garage has changed into several inner chambers. A building that resembles a small cottage stands northeast of the main house and seems to be some kind of workshop. The length of the main house runs north and south; it is a spacious domicile. I'm residing in an upstairs bedroom with one of the three bathrooms; another lies conveniently off the kitchen, and a final one serves the master bedroom. The house is full of beautiful period furniture, old and new, not to mention charming knickknacks of all types, but above all with many exceptional paintings and other artwork, some by Gail (an exceptional artist) and some by other artists. Wherever you look, you see something worth contemplating, and deriving spiritual comfort therefrom.

Paul and Gail (as guided by her artist's eye) have expended much time and effort themselves on beautifying the property, and with much love. They have planted quite a few self-contained garden plots, in particular behind the house to the east. These garden plots add enormously to the enchantment and loveliness of their three-quarter acre and possess considerable variety. In the original Persian sense the property seems to me like a self-contained paradise. All the other houses around them, well spaced from each other, also possess great botanical beauty, which serves to screen the houses from the neighbors.

On Tuesday, 22 August, we left this paradise while Paul drove us to Ron and Fran's place not quite 50 miles northwest of Portland, Maine. This mileage in addition to the 100 miles or so to cross north through the Boston area and then that little maritime corner of New Hampshire. While they overnighted in Portland, so that they could visit with a close friend formerly met in New Bedford (my hometown), I overnighted with Ron and Fran. I then spent Tuesday night, the whole of Wednesday, and Wednesday night with my only brother and sister-in-law. It resulted in a delectable interlude for us all, including Master Glenn. Paul and Gail returned Thursday morning, 24 August, visited with Ron and Fran as they all toured their rather large domicile. Then Paul, Gail, and I drove back to their home in East Sandwich.

Once we had returned, I apologized to both Paul and Gail. (Paul usually does the driving at his preference.) Had I known in advance what an ordeal it is to traverse the Boston area, I would never have asked or allowed them to do so. Although the distance is not great (probably at least 150 miles), the traffic through such an old, well-established, and well-developed area becomes a real gauntlet from Sandwich to Portland, and remains the same going back. One big ugh! Another time I'll fly from Sacramento to Portland, and then take a train or a bus from Portland to Sandwich. Much easier on all concerned, including myself, even if I need not drive the vehicle. (Argh!)

Ron at eighty-four looks excellent and has aged much better than his brother, me, Donaldo. If he has dementia (memory loss) as dictated by Alzheimer's Disease, and if nephew Jimmy had not told me in advance, I might not have been able to notice any difference. He still appears, he still is, the same fine brother whom I have known all my life, going back to the time as little kids when we would cross the street with great care (at the corner), and he would hold my hand to guide me and reassure me. With a little encouragement from me, he began to recall many things from our earlier life together before we graduated from high school, and then we went our separate ways, and in my case, really separate. Thank Goddess for Fran who looks after him!

Fran is the most remarkable eighty-five-year-old woman whom I have ever known, period, with her full and glorious head of hair. She confided in me why she has never let it grow out. It sticks out rather than hanging down. I wish that she could give me some of her hair even if I would end up looking like a Kewpie doll with top knots projecting out all around my head like a halo! Glenn at sixty-two, big, tall, and very handsome (long hair parted in the middle and pulled back into a formidable ponytail), looks to me like a teenager. Thank Goddess that he lives with his parents so that he can look after them! Such a pleasure and a relief to visit once more with all three. The rest of the family, Karen and Chris, are doing well in the Northwest, and Jimmy is also doing fine, as I could recently observe. I am still surprised at the depth and care that I can still feel for them, my brother's family.

Glenn made one great meal, a barbecue, on Tuesday night, and Fran made the other on Wednesday night. The leftovers from Monday furnished the evening meal on Tuesday. But us elders otherwise passed our time in a extended exchange of memories of our younger lives and grateful reflections on the comfortable quality of our elder existence. This wonderful interlude in Maine soon ended (as planned), Paul and Gail returned to the Fryer house in Bridgton, and then our threesome went back to Sandwich, where my own longer sojourn in New England began and continues.

What can I say about it? Interludes in paradise while in human form, at least in this dimension, are few and far between, in fact! While I shall miss my residence while with Paul and Gail at their home in East Sandwich, most of all I shall miss my hosts, my dear close friends, and my dear close relatives. They reside in the midst of an enchanted enclave that I would call upper middle class, with beautiful buildings set amid plenty of space with many trees, bushes, and vines that give privacy to the homes. No hosts could act more kindly to guests! On this profound note of gratitude I terminate this chronicle.

Catching up: register of outings 24-31 August 2017:—Wednesday, 23 August, return to Paul and Gail's from Ron and Fran's, transition during latter morning to latter afternoon.

Friday, 25 August, at the Horizon eatery and gallery, the starfish auction and art show. Gail sold her artifact to a gracious older woman who was thrilled to have it—bravo to artist and purchaser! (The starfish are giant artifacts but made with art.)

Saturday, 26 August, Gail drives Don through and around Sandwich and Cotuit, ending up at an outstanding bookshop (new, rare, and used books) owned by two friends Jim and Hank, for whom Gail worked at one time. That night Paul and Gail create a lovely birthday dinner for Jim and Hank: great chow and great companions!

Sunday, 27 August, Don treats "the three of us" at the Pilot House on the Cape Cod Canal, southeast of the Sagamore, or northern, Bridge. Excellent food and great atmosphere.

Monday, 28 August, Paul treats Don to the Sandwich Glass Museum, private establishment, a real beauty. The glass is often superb.

Tuesday, 29 August, Paul drives us three to Fairhaven and New Bedford for a tour of salient older areas in both towns, central area of Fairhaven, and the same of New Bedford. Before downtown Fairhaven, we stopped off at the house of some friends of Paul and Gail on Sconicut Neck, Ann and Butch. Ann and Gail have been friends since elementary school, early elementary! We all embarked in our two separate cars. In Fairhaven we went past the shop where Uncle Roland once had his dry-cleaning business, and then the small house (two stories) in the same block as the shop, where he lived with Aunt Fifi in one of the two upstairs flats. We also passed the Town Hall, the Millicent Library, the Congregational Church, the Unitarian Church (really a cathedral). I caught a glimpse of the extraordinary Howland Mansion, still intact with its wraparound colonnade of Ionic pillars, all of wood painted gray, set up on a mound, and with a much smaller second story set back, square, with many square contiguous windows.

New Bedford afforded us only a minimal tour. We passed the City Hall, the Public Library, parts of the older town near the docks, but only a little of County Street. Construction work on the roadbed south of the Wamsutta Club prevented us from seeing the Grinnell Mansion, the Jewish Community Center (a former whaling mansion), the Duff Mansion (all these nearby), but driving north on County Street from the Wamsutta Club we saw the glorious New Bedford High School (we also saw the magnificent Fairhaven High School, created in high Jacobean style, while we toured Fairhaven earlier). We terminated our tour of the old whaling city by driving down by the docks over the cobblestone streets, not the easiest things to drive over, and noisy! We ate lunch (a dinner really) at a great seafood eatery on Fishing Pier, Ann and Butch, Paul and Gail, and yours writerly here, courtesy of Ann and Butch.

A quiet Wednesday, I prepared for the flight back to Sacramento and then the return to Woodland, where I would be houseguarding for the Krabachers about a mile west of my cottage. On 30 August 2017 I woke up, and went downstairs about 7 or so to find a miracle. I who come from here have not experienced in more than sixty years the miracle of rain in a temperate zone with change of seasons and with all the lush greenery. What magick! A twilit low-key day, overcast, raining off and on. How the gentle rain softens everything, how nuanced, how lovely! But could I live (full sense of word) back here? I can't say. But I will say, I can now perceive why the Northeast has played such an important role in U.S. history. From early onward this area has fomented—let me emphasize that!—many people of high culture, cultivation, etc., who actively participate in their local community and in politics. How distant the West Coast seems, and in fact *is,* from the East Coast and the Northeast! Donald Trump as our new and rather crass president has activated many people to get involved in politics out of real fear of any harm that he might do!—in his case, a justified fear.

Dear Paul (Scannell) wishes me to regard him as an honorary cousin to me. However, I regard him as a full-fledged cousin, as if blood-kin, a close relative at least by marriage, in fact. Hoorah!

Thursday evening, 31 August 2017. Paul drove me to Providence with plenty of time to catch my flight via Washington, D.C., through which I passed with no delay or other trouble, thank heavens. We reached home safely. (Hallelujah!) And on time. A kind young Chinese guy let me use his cell phone to call Mike and Don, who came at once and collected me. How glad and relieved was I to see them, and I gave them each a great big hug. Dem guys izz great! I phoned Tom Krabacher at once to let him know that I was back and that we would arrange for me to come on over to their place, so that I could house-guard for them on Saturday, Sunday, and Monday—Saturday morning to sometime late afternoon Monday. I landed and found Sacramento languishing in great heat, 100° at 8:30 P.M. Such a contrast to Sandwich, Cape Cod, ranging from 70° to 50°! Eek!

Enlightenment from the Outer Dark

Wade German. *Dreams from a Black Nebula.* New York: Hippocampus Press, 2014. 134 pp. $15.00 tpb.

In case no one else in a regular print medium has expressed or emphasized it—unless a reviewer or a poet has done so in the two issues of *Spectral Realms,* Summer 2014 and Winter 2015 (magisterially edited by S. T. Joshi), and I have overlooked it—the genre of imaginative poetry (the poetry of fantasy and science fiction, if you prefer) has been undergoing not just a major renaissance but a super efflorescence as well, at least sometime since the first decade of the twenty-first century, with the founding and flourishing of Hippocampus Press under the astute guidance of owner-editor Derrick Hussey and his *vezir* S. T. Joshi. The word *assistant* or even *colleague* cannot do justice to the creative role played by Joshi not only concerning Hippocampus Press but just as much concerning the overall modern field of imaginative literature and poetry in particular. Both Hussey and Joshi have great learning and cultivation in regard to the arts and not just literary, to the benefit of all concerned.

I realize that I open myself to the charge of logrolling in praising either one or both of Messrs. Hussey and Joshi, because I have engaged with them professionally, and I have benefited from that. On the contrary, I merely state the obvious truth. No other publisher in the genre of fantasy and science fiction makes available so much new poetry, moreover in traditional form (and of polished craftsmanship), as does Hippocampus Press. Although I am gratefully aware of this contemporary cornucopia, I cannot keep up with it, however deserving of praise and meritorious it may be. I simply remain astounded, and mute with admiration, sitting on the sidelines.

Messrs. Hussey and Joshi seem to have set themselves as the main goal of Hippocampus Press the publication and promulgation of prose and poetry by Lovecraft, Ashton Smith, and other members of the Old Guard, plus the works of meritorious contemporary authors and poets, some of whom happen to continue certain aspects of the work by the Old Guard. I do know some of these people and their writings, because they appear alongside mine in *Spectral Realms.*

Sometimes I do get to know some of it in depth, an occasional volume or two, as in the present case.

Early this past spring (2015) I received (on 1 April) from Derrick Hussey an unsolicited copy of *Dreams from a Black Nebula,* by Wade German, of which volume I remain the grateful recipient. I looked it over and realized at once that Mr. German, a poet of considerable talent, had expended a great amount of care and craftsmanship on the poems included in this not so slender book, elegantly laid out and printed, of 134 pages. Single short poems have each their own page!—*comme il faut.*

German has obviously mastered meter and rime as exemplified in such demanding forms as the sonnet, the sestina, the quatrain, the pantoum, and so forth. He knows how to lay out an idea, an image, a concept, and then develop it accordingly. He has also mastered his own version of free verse and free form, but in as disciplined and impeccable a manner as that displayed in the traditional forms. Contrary to received opinion or uninformed expectation, to do good work in free verse demands almost as much dedication and skill as in the received forms.

So far I have considered German's poetry just in an external or technical fashion, hence totally inadequate. Like many poets of the weird and supernatural, he continues certain aspects and nuances in verse pioneered by Phillips Lovecraft, George Sterling, Ashton Smith, and those in prose by E. A. Poe, Robert W. Chambers, and Jack Vance. More strategically, the poetry that German mines most of all, and most importantly, belongs to himself. Despite his apparently close reading of Lovecraft's great modern sequence, the *Fungi from Yuggoth,* not to mention much of Ashton Smith's impressive corpus of poetry, German draws upon his own inventive and versatile imagination, thus fulfilling the one chief desideratum that Baudelaire himself rightfully insisted should inhere, should exist, in poetry: imagination, or (in French) *l'imaginaire.*

Rather than pontificate in some hifalutin fashion on German's poetics—a task not to my taste, and for which I have little formal aptitude—let me describe the contents of his volume and quote from the poetry here and there and throughout. He devotes as much care to his titles as to the poems themselves, so that the given title thus becomes a supplementary line—a trick, or technique, formidably exploited by poets during the nineteenth century. I need here and now to cite (from page 20) title and poem, equally evocative: the "Château Névréant." Just as the sonnet itself seems like a capsule version of "The Dark Château" by Ashton Smith, the title itself seems like a neat, lovely play on Malnéant ("A Night in Malnéant"—one of the shortest and most sublime of Smith's shorter prose fictions), which in itself means literally an "ill or evil nothingness," perhaps an aspect of the outer void (the cosmos at large) or of some locale extant in a forgotten corner of France.

Thus, through the unintentional agency of Magister German, Malnéant creates a sequel to itself, combining *never* with *ant,* to come forth as "mahl-nay-vray-AHNT." (Actually, accord to Wade himself, *névréant* is merely an anagram for *revenant.*) One could pronounce Malnéant in the French manner as "mahl-nay-AH^n"—or slightly anglicizing it, as "mahl-nay-AHNT." How I would love to read some chronicles under the heading of the Château Névréant—the narratives of which would ideally serve as a magic sesame to other worlds of beauty, splendor, and the pristine! But let me quote in full the sonnet in question:

> The cypress shadows spread a cryptic gloom
> Across the portal of the old château;
> And statues in the courtyard weirdly loom
> Like watchers on an alien plateau.
> Past crumbling stairs, dark halls and chambers seem
> Too vast and void of solace for repose
> As if supernal forces had enclosed
> This space in strange dimensions of a dream.
>
> Dark echoes out of time are anchored here.
> The portraits, armor, faded tapestries
> Would speak of baleful crimes and unknown things;
> As if a word might summon to appear
> The presence of a spectral agency
> Still bound by spells in some conjurer's ring.

Like any self-respecting craftsman working in traditional forms, German engineers his lines for maximum effects of sonority, for the ultimate music of the poetic statement itself. He does not permit his native talent or natural facility to betray him into stupidities or gaucheries. He does not fear to use "imperfect" rimes or to go against the meter briefly for an occasional foot or so. While his poems read well enough in silence, they sound even better when read or recited out loud, the ultimate test of poetry. Try it, dear reader! Read some of these poems aloud to a sympathetic friend who loves poetry, particularly poems of the fantastic and the supernatural. German skillfully utilizes repetitions in whole or in part to create haunting echoes or echo-like impressions. This dexterity comes into particular or spectacular play in his adroit pantoums—by the very nature of the form itself—some of the best that I have encountered to date. Let me quote one or more typical specimens.

THE NIGHT FOREST

I saw the shadows moving there
Like sentinels among the trees:
They stood like symbols in the air
Of long-forgotten memory.

Like sentinels anon the trees,
Arisen from the ancient night
Of long-forgotten memory,
They gathered in the pale moonlight.

Arisen out of ancient night,
As if attendant to old ways,
They gathered in the pale moonlight,
Arisen out of other days.

As if attendant to old ways,
They stood like symbols in the air
Arisen out of other days—
I knew the shadows moving there.

SHADOW AND SILENCE
—After Poe

A demon spoke to me a rune:
Strange things in time shall be unsealed
Beneath a sky without a moon,
And secret things shall be revealed.

Strange things in time shall be unsealed
Without a shadow of a sound,
And secret things shall be revealed
In silence on a shadowed ground.

Without a shadow of a sound,
An ebon sleep as smooth as glass
Like silence on a shadowed round
For many centuries shall pass.

An ebon sleep as smooth as glass
Beneath a sky without a moon
For many centuries shall pass.
And thus the demon spoke his rune.

(The last pantoum constitutes not just a beautiful tribute to Poe but specifically to his twin extraordinary poems in prose "Shadow—A Parable" and "Silence—A Fable.")

I must record and commend with a certain astonishment the becoming humility of German as a poetic practitioner vis-à-vis his immediate poetic and prose progenitors, as one who follows in their footsteps, that is, the footsteps of E. A. Poe, A. C. Swinburne, Robert W. Chambers, George Sterling, Ashton Smith, Jack Vance, and Karl Edward Wagner. The Swinburne connection in particular amazes me: few poets today would have the wit, the panache, the skill to learn from, or mimic, the poetry of Swinburne. Although echoing the rhythms and accents of Swinburne for his own purposes, going from Swinburne's diffuse to German's own succinct, the similarities between Swinburne's "Hendecasyllabics" (38 lines) and those of German's (the exact same title but with 47 lines) are very close indeed, and rather startling. We quote the first eleven lines of both poems to show the subtle transformation effected by German from Swinburne's original. Swinburne comes first, followed at once by German.

> In the month of the long decline of roses,
> I, beholding the summer dead before me,
> Set my face to the sea and journeyed silent,
> Gazing eagerly where above the sea-mark
> Flame as fierce as the fervid eyes of lions
> Half divided the eyelids of the sunset;
> Till I heard as it were a noise of waters
> Moving tremulous under feet of angels
> Multitudinous, out of all the heavens;
> Knew the fluttering wind, the fluttered foliage
> Shaken fitfully, full of sound and shadow;
> [. . .]
>
> In the month of the seventh moon of Saturn,
> I, surveying the landscape spread before me,
> Placed my feet on a path and outward wandered
> Dead dry land in the realm beyond the border,
> Crossing region of rock and giant craters
> Till I reached in the twilight open desert
> Strange red reaches of dune and desolation
> Endless, emptied of all, without oases,
> Where I saw the mirages merge with shadows,
> Flitting spectrally out among the ruins
> Half submerged in the sand—the ancient temples.
> [. . .]

Only a very good and metrically ingenious poet-craftsman could imitate so closely the essentially inimitable Swinburne, and use his narrative structure for his own creative purposes and ultimately very different ends!

But perhaps we find the unconditional apex of German's invention as well as technical skill in "The Necromantic Wine," which ranks as the longest poem in this exceptional collection, in what is as a poetic performance no less impressive than his astute and loving imitation of Swinburne in the "Hendecasyllabics."—And in fact all the more so because outwardly "The Necromantic Wine" does not appear spectacular.

The two passages quoted as epigraphs at the head of this remarkable effusion announce at once the precise tradition in which our poet continues: "A Wine of Wizardry" by George Sterling and *The Hashish Eater* by Ashton Smith. Like Sterling's poem, "The Necromantic Wine" begins quietly at sunset, as opposed to *The Hashish-Eater,* which starts with as magnificent, if not munificent, an imperial fanfare as one could imagine. But a quiet beginning can turn out as effective as any imperial summons. Without the potential threat of the dreaded anticlimax, the quiet début comfortably lures the reader into an inviting but potentially dangerous terrain.

Experiencing these visions, the informed reader perceives that German has added to his catalogue or procession of visions (all cast in a supple blank verse) much new lore gleaned from the more recent findings of astronomy and science. In vain would I quote further from this volume or from "The Necromantic Wine" (that is, beyond the title itself), a narrative longer than "Wine of Wizardry" by a third, and shorter than *The Hashish Eater* by a half. (The texture of German's poem is much lighter than that of Smith's magnum opus.) All that I can do is to urge the prospective reader to acquire the volume and savor for himself this especial but unpretentious effusion or elucubration and other poems. In writing a deliberate imitation of any pre-existing literary work, in whole or in part, the author faces at once a formidable challenge in order to succeed on his own terms. Can he avoid mere pastiche or, what is worse, unconscious parody? Our poet here succeeds in projecting his own vision, and on his own terms, and creates a worthy congener or companion to the two earlier works, the one by Sterling, the other by Smith.

Re-reading this longer poem for my own intimate perception and not force-feeding it to myself on behalf of a review, I much enjoy the visions in and of themselves. The premises are admirably stated and cogently developed. The language is always adroit, elegant, and beautiful, with the same artful combination (as exemplified so acutely in Smith, Sir Thomas Browne, Shakespeare, Marlowe, etc.) of Graeco-

Latinate polysyllables and Anglo-Saxon in one and/or several syllables. I would now rank "The Necromantic Wine" almost on the same level as "A Wine of Wizardry"—that is, in my own considered or re-considered opinion.

The fantastic or "supernatural" poets of today, those working seriously in traditional forms, have luckily found a format, a market, and a forum for their visions in Hippocampus Press, thanks to the triumvirate of Derrick Hussey, S. T. Joshi, and David E. Schultz (who typesets the material)—just as Ashton Smith as a poet posthumously has discovered his own "school" of poets and his own public following that earlier one of 1912 through 1926 (and somewhat later), that literate public in Northern California that responded to his first four poetry collections, 1912, 1918, 1922, and 1925. In the "Introduction" to his collected *Essays and Introductions* (1961), W. B. Yeats takes it upon himself to "speak the truth," clairvoyantly:

> A poet is justified not by the expression of himself, but by the public that he finds or creates; a public ready to his hand if he is a mere popular poet, but a new public, a new form of life, if he is a man of genius.

(Clearly Yeats does not mean a mass-market public produced or inspired by TV, rock 'n' roll, etc.—but by the medium of books and reading with contemplation.)

As remarkable as Eliot and Pound proved themselves as innovative poets in the 1920s and afterwards—that is, in the then modern idiom—Yeats here has pronounced the truth about poetry as a species of intuitive magic. Sometimes a great poet-genius does not find his public, his lasting public, immediately; but eventually he does discover it, after touching the lives of many poets, or the select few, of the requisite sensitivity.

A final remark. If the sorcerer who is Wade German speaks the truth in the final line of "The Necromantic Wine"—a sweet reminiscence of Ashton Smith, "This sorcerer departs!"—I sincerely hope that he will still return on occasion and give us the news from wherever he travels in the great beyond!

An Account of Donaldo's Attendance at StokerCon in Providence, R.I.

Just as I had attended the last Lovecraft Convention, the Necronomicon III during 17, 18, 19, 20 August 2017 (thanks to Derrick Hussey of Hippocampus Press and Neils Hobbs of the bookstore, H. P. Lovecraft Arts and Sciences, Providence, R.I.), said convention taking place at the Providence Biltmore and Omni Hotels, I now attended the StokerCon, during 1, 2, 3, 4 March 2018, at the same Biltmore, thanks to the kind generosity of the same Derrick Hussey, who has functioned as my chief publisher since 2007.

Although some events at this new con managed to revolve around aspects of the Lovecraft Circle—in addition to those involving Bram Stoker—I prepared myself by reviewing his best and best-known novel, *Dracula*. Whether novel or film, who knows not *Dracula?* I had read it years before, but I recalled the differences (relatively insignificant) between the novel and the first film with Bela Lugosi, more or less the same as the play of the same name, in which Lugosi made his American début on Broadway in 1931. The entry on *Dracula* in the online Wikipedia encyclopedia also refreshed my knowledge of *Dracula* and Stoker.

Also as part of my preparation, thanks to my close friend Darin Coelho, the book dealer who works at The Bookery (bookstore) in Placerville, California, east of Sacramento, I had copies of two additional novels by Stoker which I had long desired to read, *The Lair of the White Worm* and *The Jewel of Seven Stars*. Just as much as *Dracula*, these last two novels have their own special features and charms. Although Stoker might have made more of the ending in the first-cited novel, the conclusion of the other completely amazed and astonished me, so far out from the profile of the conventional novelistic finish.

Quite apart from the present Con, I have now become curious about Stoker's other novels. Even if somewhat less remarkable than *Dracula*, I sense that they are well worth experiencing. I enjoy his writing style, no less than his narrative structure or strategies. This development in terms of my own preferences does rather surprise me, since I have read comparatively little fiction during the last two or three decades, mostly poetry and histories—that is, when I have not been writing, editing and proofing, my own works. The last has become slower and more difficult with age, which has only caught up with me in the last few years, since I turned eighty-two, and incrementally since age eighty-three. My birthday is 8 September 1934.

The first part of our proceedings in the half-Stoker, half-Lovecraft Con came early on the evening of Thursday, 1 March, when we went up the steep incline of the hill by taxi to the John Hay Library of Brown University. This was about 6:00 P.M., and at 7:00 P.M. Paul Lafarge gave an hour long, well-documented lecture on H. P. Lovecraft's young friend Robert H. Barlow (1918-1951), who committed suicide at the apparent age of thirty-two following a brief but distinguished career as an anthropologist. I could but view with extreme poignance an early photo of RHB as a teenager, looking rather lost and vulnerable.

All aficionados of modern fantasy owe Barlow a huge debt of gratitude for preserving among the Lovecraft Papers at the John Hay all manner of MSS., letters, etc., from or by HPL himself, CAS, Robert E. Howard, Henry S. Whitehead, and many other distinguished contributors to *Weird Tales*. An interesting coincidence: all three of the Three Musketeers happen to share a philosophy of cosmic pessimism, despite the luxuriance of their style and vision otherwise. A quality reception followed the presentation about R. H. Barlow.

My own direct involvement in the StokerCon happened on Friday and Saturday, 2 and 3 March, and in résumé went as follows: A panel discussion, "A Haunted House with Many Poems—Horror Sub Genres," 5:00-6:00 P.M. in the Mezzanine, or nominal 2nd floor in State Suite B (actually, it seemed to be A), the issue being the need for subgenres or further subgenres. The consensus turned out equivocal.

A poetry reading or recital at H. P. Lovecraft Arts and Sciences, the bookstore owned and operated by Niels Hobbs, whom I had not met during the NecronomiCon III in August 2017, but who turned out to be an articulate and elegant younger man, and not at all the elder I had pictured in my mind last year. The bookstore is located in the Arcade, a Greek Revival building with a massive pedimented portico upheld by Ionic pillars at either end, the overall structure of two stories constructed in 1828 as the first enclosed mall in the U.S., with varied shops lining the passageway.

Niels acted as the emcee for the poetry recital, and Adam Bolivar opened the program with a good number of his mostly humorous and macabre ballads, which he presented well and with great good cheer. I followed with a half-hour or so of my own lyrics, interspersed with others by Leah Bodine Drake, Ashton Smith, George Sterling, and so forth. The audience consisted of quite a few sensitive individuals, and gave the emcee and the poets involved a warm and appreciative reception. Stanley Gemmell had planned to open for Adam and myself, but the great storm of earliest March prevented this. Instead a colorful and vivid woman poet (she seemed pretty good) did the honors.

My next panel discussion occurred on Saturday, 3 March, in the Garden Room on the Mezzanine: "The Classic Weird [Tale] in 2018." This primarily concerned how the earlier modem masters of F&SF such as Arthur Machen, Lord Dunsany, CAS, HPL, etc., established a tradition that "illuminated strange, bleak, nihilistic world views." Their work has provided much of the foundation for the authors of the so-called New Weird. Once again, the conclusion or consensus turned out as equivocal.

Sunday, 4 March, I had as a free time, and so I did a variety of things: I began this account, I wandered here and there, talked with the Con attendees, spent much time with Derrick at the display of his books, that is, of Hippocampus Press, as I signed as many copies of my own titles published by him, etc. While at his display, I also signed copies of my books to various individuals and palavered with them, all quite gratifying.

In the early afternoon Adam Bolivar rented a car to drive in order to see a close friend in Framingham; but first, with author Jonathan Thomas acting as the expert backseat guide, Adam drove us to the cemetery that holds the Lovecraft family tombstones, including HPL's own. We arrived at the cemetery and parked not far from the metal-barred double gate. Alas, due to the vehement nor'easter that struck at least much of the Massachusetts coast (including Cape Cod), many trees and branches had collapsed onto the cemetery grounds—the graveyard was closed, with a police car parked just beyond the right-hand wrought-iron gate. No sneaking into the cemetery, it was obvious. We WILL try again on another occasion at another convention.

Thus the highlight of this aborted attempt to see HPL's grave turned out to be the long route to the graveyard thoughtfully indicated by Jonathan, covering an extensive territory, a plateau apparently raised high above sea level. Providence is big, Providence is beautiful, with many big beautiful homes, mansions, bungalows, and somewhat smaller middle-class homes. Applause to Jonathan for the grand tour that he de facto arranged!

The other highlight was the visit to the home that Jonathan shares with his beautiful wife Angel, who is an angel just like Jonathan himself. But first we visited a charming and surprising bookstore owned by a friend of Jonathan's, the place going by the name of the Paper Nautilus. The owner is a petite and enchanting lady, Kristin. The main floor of the shop is an attractive and well-illuminated space with the bookcases and the books themselves invitingly arranged. The big surprise takes the form of a larger basement floor even more attractive, and packed with books of all kinds but all in good to great shape.

Then at his invitation we visited Jonathan and Angel's lovely house, more spacious on the inside than what one might reckon from the outside: three or four rooms downstairs and four or five rooms upstairs with a bathroom, as well as a half-bathroom downstairs. Their house is a very pleasant and fun abode with many little collections of cute odds and ends. It all makes for a warm domestic ambiance with warm and friendly hosts. Once again, as at the NecronomiCon III, I had a wonderful conversation with Angel, once a café singer in Manhattan. I fell in love at once with Bug (formerly Bud), the cutest Boston Terrier that I had seen in years, since I as co-owner had enjoyed Tippy and Suzie as my sweet and near constant companions.

Today, Monday, 5 March 2018, all I have done is to prepare to leave, to pack up, and then return home to Cape Cod. Much later! Tuesday morning, 6 March, 2018. It seems that I might be returning to Providence no later than by the next NecronomiCon in August 2019, 15–18, thus close to 20 August 1890, his birthday, but I may return earlier, thanks to dear Niels Hobbs of the HPL bookstore at the Arcade. It appears that he is an aficionado of DSF among many others—I am in awe (and disbelief) of anyone in awe of DSF—huh? I might also hie me to Manhattan to help celebrate "St." Joshi's 60th birthday under the aegis of Derrick Hussey and Hippocampus Press. Buses do go from the Cape to both Providence and Manhattan. We'll see!

One of the chief pleasures of attending any Con remains the opportunity to meet people—interested, as passionately and as obsessively as one's own self, in a certain subject or phenomenon: in our case, divers literary genres of F. and S. F. Another of these chief pleasures remains the discovery of other people articulate, savvy, and cultivated in their passions and preferences, that is, overall cultured folkses. I was able to share obsessions with many new friends as well as with many old friends at the NecronomiCon III, or earlier at other Cons. So be it!

In the Footsteps of the Masters

Henry J. Vester III. *Of Mist and Crystal: Selected Poetry.* Fungoid Press/VirtualBookworm.com Press, 2015. 74 pp. $16.96 hc.

It is obvious that poet Henry J. Vester III is at least a literary connoisseur, as his hardcover book of poetry reveals the lore and appreciation of the modern masters of prose and poetry in the genre(s) of literature involving a general fantasy and science-fiction perspective, as the poet himself reveals in his "Author's Forward" [*sic*]: H. P. Lovecraft, Robert E. Howard, George Sterling, Joseph Payne Brennan, Stanley McNail, Ambrose Bierce, Richard L. Tierney, Ann K. Schwader, and (above all) Clark Ashton Smith, otherwise Klarkash-Ton. The author himself bears witness that he nourished his first tastes in poetry (apart from, but including, E. A. Poe) on the following volumes: *Dark of the Moon,* the anthology of weird and macabre poetry edited by August Derleth (1947); the later and similar volume *Fire and Sleet and Candlelight,* also edited by Derleth (1961); and the *Collected Poems* of H. P. Lovecraft, likewise edited by Derleth (1963). The anthologist-editor published all three volumes through his publishing firm Arkham House (Sauk City, Wisconsin). The present volume has two appreciative and exceptional introductions, the first by W. H. Pugmire, the second by Gregorio Montejo. Henry Vester well deserves the praise and elucidation, the lore and learning, imparted by these introductions.

This first book of poetry, and also the author's first solo volume of any type, is a small handsome hardcover, a little gem of production (5.25 × 8.25″), with a handsome cover by Allen Koszowski, a practiced artist of the weird and fantastic. In addition to the three prefaces, the volume contains twenty-four poems in verse and ends with a poem in prose, as well as with "Some Notes on the Poems" (these are helpful) assembled by the poet himself—explaining and identifying people and places in a playful manner. The back cover gives us basic information "About the Author," now a retired social worker who has worked as a family therapist near or at Santa Rosa, California, but most recently in a large community mental health center at Klamath Falls, Oregon.

Mr. Vester writes in variety of styles and forms whether traditional or non-traditional, clearly and straightforwardly. As noted by Gregorio Montejo, he commands "a dark yet sinuous line," no less than a broad range of imagery and allusion, both of which come to the fore in the tributes to various poetic masters. Chilling moments abound in the poems themselves, but succinctly, as in the poetry of Ambrose Bierce and Leah Bodine Drake. (Relative to some hunters who go exploring where they should not, "In the tower was horrible laughter.")

The poet first strikes the note of lonely and macabre reflection in the opening morceau, "Medicine Wind," and sustains it throughout all nine stanzas:

> I sat this eve alone
> In an unfrequented place,
> Disdaining solace or companion
> In the hour of my reflection.

He has also mastered a subtle allusiveness as presented in the poem's second stanza, where he refers to the sun and the moon respectively:

> And as the desert's master
> Drowned himself again in bloodied sands,
> Its mistress arose in haste,
> As a lover tardy to a secret tryst.

The final two stanzas resume the poem's metaphysical depths in an expert way:

> All through the night the song went on,
> Oblivious of any ear.
> And all the threads of my spirit
> It untangled, reweaving in its own image.
>
> And as the master rose again,
> I suddenly remembered, and
> The spirit wind flew, laughing, away,
> Salting again my bones with sandy tears.

Mixed in with all the macabre reflections, often with startling surprise endings, Mr. Vester reveals a very nice sense of humor, as in one of the tributes to HPL, "An Old Gentleman Seeks Professional Help." The tribute to pictorial artist Gervasio Gallardo, "Visionary," is no less notable in its precise and serious register of the covers that Gallardo painted for Ballantine's Adult Fantasy series. The poet proves again his sense of humor in "A Yuletide Encounter," where he does an adroit and clever take-off of "A Visit from St. Nicholas," otherwise "The Night Before Christmas," and to hilarious effect. Other tributes to HPL appear in "The Bells of R'lyeh," "Dagon's Halls," and "The Scroll of Alhazred." Mr. Vester strikes perhaps his deepest notes or tones in the tributes to Clark Ashton Smith, "To the Shade of Klarkash-Ton" and "Klarkash-Ton Walks at Midnight." In the first cited poem HJV's use of the true second person singular seems especially appropriate and moving. The second piece of homage turns out just as lovely and serious, a touching *jeu d'esprit.*

We can point to other titles and tributes, notably the one to "Ray" (the master fantaisiste Ray Bradbury), but rather than that, and further quotations from Mr. Vester's poetry, we would urge the serious reader to obtain a copy of *Of Mist and Crystal* and con the poems' individual morceaux. Altogether then, we can heartily recommend this book, this unequivocally delectable book, to the literary connoisseur and lover of imaginary poetry. And we have almost forgotten to add that the concluding prose-poem, "Of Ancient Glory" (4.5 pp.), is a rare and profoundly moving work of art worthy of Lord Dunsany and Ashton Smith!

One final note. The author in his preface lists various poets and other writers who have influenced and liberated his poetic vision, his inner landscape of dream and revery. We repeat them here: Edgar Allen Poe, H. P. Lovecraft, Robert E. Howard, George Sterling, Joseph Payne Brennan, Stanley McNail, Ambrose Bierce, Richard L. Tierney, Ann K. Schwader, and Clark Ashton Smith (shades of Poe and Sterling intensified!), and probably others as well (but unregistered). This quality is something that he shares with C. Ashton Smith. It relates to something fundamental to style (or subject), and that remains the *tone* of the language carefully sifted and selected by the poet (HJV III), a quality as impeccable as Ashton Smith's own, or (in

French) that of Baudelaire. On those grounds alone Henry Vester finds himself among the modern elect as registered by himself.

We cannot resist quoting in full one more poem, or so.

ECHOES

Echoes of a winter wind
Whisper within an ancient skull—

Stir memories of loves long lost,
The more hungered for because
They never were.

AWAKE

Who treads so softly 'round
That none but ghosts of bats in attic dark
Discern the steps which scarcely tramp the snow?
I lie awake by single candle's glow,
And dare not sleep for fear of that
Which unprotected dreams may show.

Musings Philosophical and Religious

Alan Gullette. *Reviving a Dead Priest.* Oakland, CA: translucent books, 2018. 120 pp. $9.95 tpb.

As an elder in the community of poets who have contributed to the "Hippocampus Press Library of Poetry" (thus under the name of the seahorse as tutelary beast), it has been our great pleasure to watch new figures in the poetic genre of fantasy and science fiction, or science fantasy, emerge, grow, develop. Some we know as personal friends, and others at least as cordial acquaintances, encountered at conventions and similar events; some over the long term, and others only briefly (but significantly) so far.

Thus we have long known, or known of, Richard Tierney, Ann K. Schwader, and Alan Gullette; now more recently Ashley Dioses, K. A. Opperman, and Wade German; a few poets only through correspondence. Alan Gullette in addition has functioned as our long-term collaborator, without whose irreplaceable help some dozen books of ours could never have seen print—his indispensable help as a computer specialist.

Besides having books published by other houses, Gullette has appeared as part of those writers made public by Hippocampus Press under the enlightened aegis of owner-editor Derrick Hussey centered in New York City: in Gullette's case with *Intimations of Unreality*. This poet and author has built up an impressive corpus of literary works over the years. We here append the chief titles. *Another Eucharist* (1995); *From a Safe Distance* (2000); *Intimations of Unreality* (2012); *The Lighthouse Above the Graveyard* (with John Allen, 2016); *The Adventures of Franco Corelli* (2017); *I Grew These Hueless Clouds in the Dreary South* (2017); *Short Shrift* (2017); *Pantaleon* (2018). Most of these are poetry, with some as a mixture of poetry and prose. While they are basically free verse in free form, Gullette yet presents his poems in highly disciplined lines formed into regular verse paragraphs. The overall effect: liberated traditional, but still modern, very much so.

We have here now for inspection and experiencing at length a copy of his latest book of poetry, *Reviving a Dead Priest*. To give it overall shape, Gullette has organized the volume with the story-line of a religious teacher or priest. This guru dies and leaves as a legacy only his poems. His followers are perplexed as to what to do, but they have evidently given the poems to Alan as a sympathetic amanuensis and/or editor, who has now presented them as the book in hand. This all shapes up into a plausible scenario for the volume's raison d'être. Establishing the tone of the poetry in the collection, on the back of this trade handsome trade paperback (which features the striking portrait, a piece of art, showing some Far Eastern monk or priest), Alan quotes from the Japanese Buddhist priest Dogen Zenji: "He has plucked out the eye of the buddha ancestors and sat down inside that eye."

It is a generous collection, containing over seventy poems, including three pages of aphorisms as the antepenultimate selection that includes quite a few fascinating insights and pensées. The author, also the editor, has arranged the mostly short poems into the following sections: "Death and Life," "Initiation," "Of Seeming and Being," "Light from the East," "Reflections on Time," "Tabernacle Fire," "Five Prayers and a Psalm," "Revival," "The End." Short poems and short lines abound, often aphoristic in thought and feeling. Because, as the titles above indicate, the poet deals with subjects of the greatest weight and often fear, the presentation favored by the author comes across as light-hearted and thus reduces the dread and fear often aroused by such topics.

In this way the poetry becomes accessible and easy of approach, and the author maintains an amazing directness and clarity. By such a method he avoids needless confusion and complexity, a remarkable accomplishment in view of the heaviness of the subject matter. Thus he shows that if he has indeed imbibed some of the wisdom of the Far East, especially that of India. This wisdom probably shows up best in the longer poems: "The Blood Sutra," "Pontus and the Nagas," "Samantabhadra Takes a Nap," and "Tabernacle Fire." These four narratives are all wisdom fables, demonstrating much play, whimsy, irony, and humor. In fact, this characteristic sense of humor, not blatant but comfortable and relaxed, animates much of the volume, as do the title and the book's overall concept. Who would wish to revive a dead priest?—except metaphorically.

As the final stanza of "The Dead Priest" expresses it succinctly: "If the priest's unspoken words / Escape the funeral pyre, / Who will hear them?" (The poem's own quotation marks.) But let us quote a little bit from here and there throughout the volume to give the reader a feeling for the poet's unique sense of existential fun! (These quotes are mostly the conclusions of the pieces from which we cite.)

From "The Face of Doom":

> There are two things
> > that I can say of him:
> He is fixed in purpose,
> > and his grip is firm . . .

From "Funeral Rites":

> A great day to be alive!
> A great day to die!
> A great day to be buried!
> A great day to be revived!

From "Seer":

> Who has borne the burden of beauty
> Back from the realms sublime?

An entire brief poem, *"Poiema"* [Greek, a thing made]:

> Time lends Life's Spinner
> and descends
>
> Three eyes see I
> what is
> What could be
>
> One cries with sorrow
> One laughs with joy
> One sees

From "Incantation:":

> Life exists not in time
> But in the moment
> The moment exists not in time
> But in space

From "The Universe Breathes":

> Take a breath—
> The universe is breathing!
> Take a breath
> And hold it still . . .

From "The Fundament":

> In everything, there is nothing;
> In nothing, there is everything.
> That's the fundamental truth.

In closing the section of direct quotations, we can do no better than to cite in full the two last poems in the collection. The first is "Giving Thanks":

I would like to thank
My mother and father
—and all the mothers and fathers before them—
For bringing me *here*.

I would also like to thank
Mother Earth and Father Sky,
Brother Sun and Sister Moon,
The Milky Way and all the Stars—
And the Big Bang.

And last, but not least,
I would like to thank

The Big Silence
That surrounds it all.

The second is "The Master Appeared":

> The master appeared to me in a dream.
>
> "There is precious little that you can do
> To revive a dead priest. But the living—
> *They* may have a chance."

Thus in many of these truly metaphysical poems the poet expresses diverse musings and fancies that many of us have entertained at times, but he has rendered us, poets and non-poets alike, a real service in doing so in such a lucid and accessible manner. We personally find this volume a godsend or a cosmos-gift of clarity in terms of the ongoing existential maelstrom and confusion. And for that we thank the author for *Reviving a Dead Priest*. Religion is not dead either officially or unofficially! But religious thought, to be genuine, must include a healthy skepticism.

All that we can do here, as well as with previous books, is to urge the enlightened reader to seek further enlightenment as purveyed in this enlightening volume. How the master or the messenger on the book's front cover appears beautifully dark-skinned, he who brings the message of enlightenment with its promise of spiritual light! This book exercised a positively therapeutic effect on us: and as experienced in strict sequence over the course of a single day of concentrated reading, it changed our consciousness. We cannot ask for anything more than that from any book, and especially from a book of poetry. The sense of fantasy and linguistic play holds high carnival in this volume!

The Miscellaneon

Poems in Verse and Prose

DEDICATED
to two special relatives
as well as special friends
GAIL AND PAUL SCANNELL.

Contents

Apollo-Ganymede 193
Only Fifty Times Removed 194
Cet au-delà That Lies Beyond 195
No Escape from Vehicular Mobility 196
The Ministers of Chance 197
The Eden-Paradise That Haunts Our Undersoul 198
O Brave New World of Faerie Lands Forlorn 199
No One's Realm 200
Time Bomb 201
Some Lordly Helmet 202
An Achaemenian Munificence 203
Another Spenserian Stanza-Sonnet Once Again 204
Moonlight Mood 205
A Rendezvous in a Newer Carthage 206
The Black Swan with the Scarlet Bill 207
Old New Bedford, and Even Older 208
An Offering as from Afar 210
An Unknown Isle in 2017? 211
A Vagrant Vessel Plying Here and There 212
Return to Paradise Lost 213
A Victorian Poem in Redwood 214
An Island Is an Independent Realm 216
A Futuristic Icon of an Easter Island Head 217
Some Little Windows on the World 218
Winter Scene 219
Kaleidoscopic Odyssey 221
    Change Is as Change Insists 231
    The Miracle of Palm Trees in the Dusk 232
    The Unicorn Looks at the Lady from Afar 233
    Squirrels at Play 236

    An Experiment in Variation 237
    The Uplet and the Cuplet 238
    No More of Majesty 239
    Snowfall 240
    A Fellow Creature on Our Planet 242
    Needments and Oddments 243
    The Elder Daemon 244
Notes, by Dlanod Yendis 247
Afterthoughts 251
Postscriptum: Cape Cod and Canal 253

Apollo-Ganymede

(For Stanley Gemmell)

He seemed a messenger, as of the gods,
The dark exotic youth, whose loveliness
He used for something else than ends and odds.
The looks, the voice, he used for nothing less
Than poetry, the play, the thought, the guess,
Stage-whispered, or declared out loud, but loud.
He chose which words or images to stress,
With stance and mien direct, but kind and proud:
His faith seemed patent, even if not otherwise avowed.

One cannot ask much more than this of any poet-bard,
A stance uncompromising, but audacious and unbowed—
Against such art, once grasped, there can exist no potent guard.

As for Zeus or Apollo, I would rather shun than heed:
Rather would I befriend Antinous or Ganymede!

Only Fifty Times Removed

(With thanks to Jesse Allen
for pointing the datum out to the poet)

If we are all no more than fifty times removed
One from another, then we make up one big kin,
But still, how far from our inception have we moved!

What supernature's force, disclosed, might we begin
To wield, on loan from angel, daemon, god, or djinn,
But only thus to get along in peace and calm?!

We need more patience, rather than a paladin,
Much more than we might need misgiving, fear, or qualm:
It bodes far better to give balm, than rather to embalm!

A positive commandment, and an overall good rule:
Greet all and sundry hominids with bow, smile, and salaam:
Better a cautious wise man, than a dead and stupid fool.

Treat everyone at least at first with due respect:
It is no more than what we might ourselves expect.

Cet au-delà That Lies Beyond

The horns that call from Spenser's *Faerie* lond,
Or from John Keats his Fairylands forlorn,
Might they perhaps still come forth from beyond?
Cet au-delà, that Otherwhere, forsworn
By some, embraced by others, *is* that bourne
In some companion cosmos, but unseen:
Those worlds that none can prove, nor yet suborn,
Worlds within worlds, before, behind, between—
Spheres within spheres above, what entity could contravene?

Empearled, begemmed, a cosmos evermore unfurled,
A cosmos that lies parallel, sensed but unseen—
The trumpet-clarions announce yet one more world.

Might they perhaps still come forth from that great beyond,
The clarions that blow—how far—from Spenser's *Faerie* lond?

No Escape from Vehicular Mobility

(A modest complaint)

"And later times things more unknown shall show."
—Edmund Spenser, *The Faerie Queene,* II: Proem: III.

Although they cannot quite climb up a steeple,
The horseless carriages drive everywhere:
By now they must outnumber all the people!
And though they move with caution and with care,
Their noxious fumes!—they plague our common air,
And plague our sight and sense with lethal breath:
Thus this effluvium so less than fair,
This ghastly smell whose fragrance lingereth,
This might someday perhaps cost all of us our death!

From campfires, hearths, and factories,
    the carbon thus released,
As far back as the long reign of
    the first Elizabeth,
Now threatens all of us far more
    than monster dragon-beast!

As uttered elsewhere, everything is linked:
    What good our smarts, or our nobility?
If we succeed in making us extinct?!
    So what price then is this mobility?

The Ministers of Chance

(With apologies to C. Ashton Smith,
and to Al Capp for the phrase from *Li'l Abner*)

The splendor and the transience of thine hour
Are one, one only hour, thou "hoomin bean"—
Within that straitened compass must thou flower!
But yet, so far, there is no end foreseen
In spite of this apocalyptic spleen
Which we now sense in humankind at large.
Protected by what nimbus or what sheen,
Might we shoot at some target or some targe,
Secure in some oasis on what margent or what marge?

Our arrowed thoughts we shoot at random, as we please,
As from big pipe we take deep breath, or supercharge—
Is this our own free choice, or decadent unease?

The House of Chance looms larger than the Ministry of Law,
A fact that we should ponder with true piety and awe!

The Eden-Paradise That Haunts Our Undersoul

To find a novel blossom in some blossom-bourne,
Which could somehow combine the orchid and the rose:
Its non-discovery could make us laugh or mourn.
Species do not combine like that, but whoso knows
What might occur where tropic trees and vines enclose
What prodigies of bloom that no one can surmise?
Because, always ahead of us as Nature goes
About her basic chores, always can she surprise,
Can she amaze, our conscious view, right there
                              before our eyes.

Was it with blossoms that our kind first sensed the soul,
To tell a thing's pure essence, under any guise,
To see the kinship with the soul, the undersoul?

And is that why we hanker back to Eden-Paradise?—
To which we would return, if but we could,
                              and in a trice!

O Brave New World of Faerie Lands Forlorn

O brave new world of Faerie lands forlorn,
But always based on older worlds of dream,
This impulse is of its own self pure-born!
What outré tune or melody or theme
Could celebrate the Abbey of Theleme,
That ideal place of living civilized?
Who are the servants in that choice regime?—
Save an elite deserving to be prized—
Where thus together they as one and all have equalized.

Ideal response in ideal state, this Abbey of Theleme,
But it is purely fabulous, and thus hypostatized—
So, Shangri-La upon Theleme, or on an earlier dream.

Does each Utopia trace
                      on back to Platonist Atlantis?—
That Eden-Paradise
                      that does not falter to enchant us?

No One's Realm

Where can we find, pray tell, some common ground
Where thought and poetry might co-exist,
Some equable terrain that has no bound?
Or must we function as an alchemist,
To demonstrate some thanks, a eucharist,
Before we find that space that no one owns?
Or is it ever lost as in a mist,
Or buried underneath a cairn of bones,
Or underneath a heap pf rocks, or yet a pile of thrones?

Must we search out this place in far and foreign lands?
Can we still find this common ground that no one owns?
This realm that lies beyond our grasp, beyond our hands?

This locale where the wild wind shudders, howls, or moans,
Or where some pious hymn a vagrant breeze intones?

Time Bomb

The human population: it would seem
To expand with the speed as of a train,
A high-speed train, a runaway express,
Or thus it would appear, like nowadays.
Is there an engineer who operates
The engine car?—is nobody in charge?—
As the train flies like a bat out of hell—
Unstoppable save by some uttermost crash?
The human race seems as if on a crash course with itself!

Unless we manage to trek out onward among the stars,
A dénouement devoutly to be wished—let it occur!—
What shall we do with all these extra people everywhere?

Where are the jobs, the social services, for all of them?
Are all such questions now quixotic or irrelevant?

Some Lordly Helmet

> "the conquered rust
> Of lordly helms made equal in the dust."
> —George Sterling, "A Wine of Wizardry"

The Atlantean helm still stood upright,
Deep in that intermidmost cave, somehow—
Crowned with tridented crown, with ghostly light.
Some commandant had worn it, anyhow,
To whom a vast force would have made the bow,
To implement what seemed expedient.
What does the lowly soldier need avow,
Homage to whom?—what prime ingredient,
If he survives?—upwards to move, upon the gradient?

What of that lowly soldier, and what of that commandant?
Vain speculation, given time's supreme emollient
To wear away the very dust, and all things that enchant.

But still the Atlantean helmet has itself survived,
Deep in that cavern, where it still stands free, nor ever gyved.

An Achaemenian Munificence

Persepolis, the annual durbar, the vernal or vertumnal aequinox.

The hundred columns of the treasure-hall stood firm,
The floor one giant square, with other squares inside.
With central aisles kept free, where did the Great King sit?—
Enthroned among this wealth, as piled in other aisles,
The side aisles cornerwise? or in the midst thereof?—
At one end of a central aisle, in inner-sanctum style?
The satraps and embassadors—they came with gifts
Of greatest prize and price, of great art or design;
They brought them in with high respect, in pride, in dignity.

Perhaps the Great King smiled, nodding in recognizance,
Approval to be wished, and cherished, once evinced,
By those who had travailed in fact from far away.

What treasure-troves did Alexander Magnus not discover?—
What prodigies of art, amassed long-term, did he not find?

Another Spenserian Stanza-Sonnet Once Again

(Surrealistical mélange)

As if they waxed in some odd stanza-sonnet;
The ostrich, and the ibex, and the ibis;
A scheme of suchlike rime-words laid upon it;
The triad of Osiris, Horus, Isis;
A bolt of dazzling cloth cut on the bias;
The sunrise, and the sunset, and the nox;
A mix of ice cream, sherbet, ice, and ices;
The oceans with their endless organ-vox;
Likewise like tides the hours that make unceasing ebb and flux:

What fiat makes the where, the when, the how, the why?
What makes the point of all of it, what makes the crux?
Might we make sure, or ascertain, with wedjet eye?

The triad of Osiris, and of Horus, and of Isis
Reiterates: the ostrich, and the ibex, and the ibis.

Moonlight Mood

(A memory of Sandy Neck, Cape Cod)

The night lay quiet, and the moon shone full
Upon the stretch of silent beach, and where
The dunes, the sand hills, lift up beautiful:
The grassy mounds would seem, albeit bare,
To stretch forevermore, foreverwhere,
Like some Saharan mini mountain range:
This place might cause a poet to despair—
This neck of land, so marvellous and strange—
How into simple words its awe could interchange:

A landscape, a sandscape, as if perhaps from Otherwhere,
Was this a sacred place to native folk, remote from change?
Or so they might have thought, that none or nothing
                                          could impair?

So far, their thought, their hope, appears to have prevailed,
In spite of *the* developers, before whom much hath failed.

A Rendezvous in a Newer Carthage

Would you not meet me in Cartagena de las Indias?—in that marvelous Old City with its fantasticated elder buildings, and with those lofty, massive, and incredible walls, *las murallas,* that arose long agone as if by magic (even if by the labor of many slaves), and at the command of Felipe Dos of España, ensconced in his cathedral-palace-fortress, the Escorial, outside Madrid—so very different, so very far on the other side of the Ocean Sea, the Atlantic. How cold and how different from his tropical treasure-town of the Indies far to the west!—with her palm trees, her gardens, her plazas or public squares, not to leave unmentioned the lush and exuberant verdure surrounding that once great metropolis. Phoenix-like it arose after every siege, every pillage and plunder, every storm of fire and destruction. To this day the Old City remains unique, impressive, beautiful.

But let us not meet there during the heavy rains or the greatest heat. Let us find shelter at some inn or in some sweet and modest hotel where we may also take our meals. The town yet remains its centuried self as it was when we traveled there in our young manhood, footloose and fancy free before all the attachments of maturity, marriage, children, and then finally divorce for both of us, no less than the freedom to travel once again as in our youth. What do you say? Write me as early as possible. Let us plan a new adventure!

The Black Swan with the Scarlet Bill

(Dedicated to Leah Bodine Drake, in memoriam)

>The black swan with the scarlet bill:
>From what shore does he hail, pray tell?
>From way down under—if you will,
>The antipode—but not from hell,
>>The black swan with the scarlet bill.

>With black unglossy featherage
>Full-smooth as any nap or suede,
>Full-fledged as with an equipage,
>So this bird paddles unafraid,
>>The black swan with the scarlet bill.

>Lordly, exotic, and serene,
>The avian glides across the pool;
>Beautiful, and composed in mien,
>He keeps an air aloof and cool,
>>The black swan with the scarlet bill.

>Caught in some eddy of the pond,
>A-swim, a-swirl, a-swoon, a-sheen,
>As in a wavelet from beyond,
>Naught has this bird of base or mean,
>>The black swan with the scarlet bill.

Old New Bedford, and Even Older

During my teenage years, above all during the late 1940s and early 1950s, thus during my four years in high school (from the time I was thirteen until just before I turned eighteen)—whenever I was not preoccupied with my all-involving studies during the school year, and then with summer camp or odd jobs during the warmer weather (June through September)—I would sometimes employ my weekends (the occasional Sunday) to explore much of New Bedford along preeminent County Street, with its old and picturesque elm trees whose antient branches created Gothic arches over the thoroughfare, thus discovering and re-discovering the old mansions built in the heyday of the whaling period, most of them constructed of wood, but a small number of brick or quarried stone, usually granite, and the major part of them surmounted by the cupolas with widow walks around them. Most of these houses featured a principal block of abode (two stories plus attic) with a good-sized wing attached behind it.

Gradually I gravitated more and more down New Bedford's overall ridge toward the eastern end of William Street. Here lifts up the lesser eminence of Johnnycake Hill with the Seamen's Bethel at the top on the west of the street and to the east the Jonathan Bourne Whaling Museum done in brick and designed in proper Georgian style. The other and older buildings had been made out of wood like the big sailing ships.

While I would prowl around the general area of the nonpareil museum, I moved on down closer and closer to the margin of the older docks with their cobblestoned streets and their warehouses, some of them constructed in brick. I began to look at some of the elder buildings and to notice that some of them had begun their existence by serving as good-sized family houses, if not in fact mansions, but sometimes later used as business depots or warehouses, the overall style suggesting Georgian or post-Georgian. All at once, like a lightning flash, it dawned on me that the earliest mansions of the maritime gentry had lifted up not very far from the docks and the overall waterfront, thus with the wharves, the ships, and the businesses that catered to the ships, their building, their repairing, and their supplying.

As the city prospered and expanded, it gradually moved up the extensive north-and-south ridge along which (as along the Acushnet River) the community developed. Eventually it attained the summit of the ridge marked by County Street and the later generation of mansions, the typical dwellings of the main whaling period, say, the 1840s up through the Civil War. Although battered by that war and by various Arctic disasters, the whaling industry managed somehow to endure on into the third decade of the twentieth century, the 1920s—quite a feat.

An Offering as from Afar

Upon that further shore, which we may never reach,
What would we do if we could make a foothold there,
Upon some arctic strand, upon some tropic beach?
Better the latter choice, for food and warmth and air,
For dulcet atmosphere, like breath from Otherwhere
A gentle wind from off the waves can only please,
Mixing its blunt and salt-sea-sharp aromas there
With those of balsams from some unknown tropic trees,
Like mingling far-off music with plain, local melodies:

The three kings who came bearing frankincense and myrrh
Could not bring anything more likely to appease
Than paradisal balms as something to confer:

Might there be music like to myrrh and frankincense
In strangeness and in subtlety and in eloquence?

An Unknown Isle in 2017?

Looking back in time, let us remember what we can, but without our marine charts and ocean maps, so painstakingly recorded by generations of mariners! We had sailed somewhere into the eastern reaches of the Caroline Islands, and therefore somewhere in the Western Pacific Ocean, some 1000 miles northeast of New Guinea. We had already visited Pohnpei to the northwest and then Kosrae to the southeast, some 300 miles intervening between them, and some 500 miles or so north of the Equator. The distances in the Pacific basin often turn out vast, even when traversed by modern jet plane, never mind by sailboat, or by big cruise ship.

For some reason we decided to sail back from the megalithic ruins of Leluh on Kosrae to visit again the far more extensive ruins of Nan-Madol on Pohnpei. We were sailing in our miniature clipper ship, some 100 feet long with four masts, but otherwise regularly sized relative to our human scale. An unknown, fairly large volcanic island, not on our charts and maps, had suddenly appeared out of the ocean! In great excitement we reached the locale, and anchored in a tranquil harbor at sunset. We did not land, choosing to wait until the morning to disembark. But when we woke up the next day, the island had vanished! Had we all suffered a collective hallucination? We never sighted the island again.

A Vagrant Vessel Plying Here and There

The good ship called the *Miscellaneon*
Can transport more abundant cargo than
That other ship, the *Necronomicon:*
Our ship's nocturnal beacons beam, and span—
Better than any other vessel can—
A continent, or yet the seven seas:
No limit for our freight, nor any ban,
To anyone who might possess the keys,
Some dexterous captain who could navigate the Cyclades:

Meanwhile, what of those other ships?
    They also ply their trade
From place to place, from isle to isle,
    and readily, with ease;
They transport food, goods, medicine, or any other aid:

We do not trade in gods or daemons,
    they come on board as contraband;
They come along like unseen lemans,
    but easier to keep on land.

Return to Paradise Lost

When from our little clipper ship we first spied the unknown, fairly large volcanic island, our hearts collectively leapt up. How could they not have done so? Some thirty miles or so away, the expanse one can perceive at a distance on the seemingly flat surface of a calm body of water, the isle appeared as the perfect embodiment of a Polynesian dream-locale. There it manifested on the horizon, as if having just emerged out of the ocean. We looked at each other in dumbfoundment. We reached the isle at sunset, and anchored in a tranquil harbor, behind an arm of land. After excited palaver we decided to wait until the morning to land and explore, when we would be fresh and refreshed.

The locale appeared to be a classic Pacific Ocean island with a volcano placed more or less in the middle, and with many palm trees highlighting the lavish verdure everywhere, covering the terrain from near the beach all the way to the top of, and over, the extinct volcano. Rather strangely no campfires or other lights betrayed a native population. Was the isle uninhabited, as well as unknown? No bird or other cries betrayed a native fauna.

Sometime just before dawn the island vanished as mysteriously as it had emerged. Utterly dumbfounded, we could only discuss the phenomenon as we continued our voyage back to Pohnpei and Nan-Madol.

A Victorian Poem in Redwood

(The Gable Mansion, Woodland, California, 1885)

I

The lordly structure stands beautiful and proud, on its own very large corner property, along a street with other big and handsome family houses. It is not the usual stereotypically Victorian horror mansion fit for a Halloween Hollywood nightmare. It is not a house painted black or dark gray, alive with turrets and towers and finials, and perchance endowed here and there with stained-glass windows, which otherwise might suggest some unorthodox Gothic cathedral, given over to Satanic rituals, Black Masses, or possibly darker ceremonies.

Here no heavy draperies of dark brocade hang on the side at the tall windows—draperies dyed in mauve, gray, black, or a rich unsaturated brown—draperies that allow but little illumination inward upon the massive and weighty furniture that could not seem less ponderous. This mansion does not sport either gewgaws or gargoyles or furbelows, or any other strange details. And yet it boasts the best of the high Victorian style, that named Italianate.

II

No, this mansion is not part of that darker Victorian domestic vision, no matter how authentically Victorian it remains otherwise on the inside and out. Along with full cellar and attic, it boasts two full stories and a slightly lower third story. Whoever the architect, he had obviously rare taste and imagination, and contrived a soberly (or chastely) spectacular Victorian palace, with high porch, tall windows, and many little balconies at all the levels, not to overlook one large but graceful gable at the top and on the front, a gable that features a commanding stained-glass window. The house is painted overall in a light beige, and with most of the trim in white. Despite its size, the structure creates a general effect full of light and lightness, the grace and graciousness of another age.

III

Centrally located on its own extensive lot at the northeast corner of Cross and First Streets half a dozen blocks south of Woodland's Main Street, the overall structure lifts up, a solid and substantial towerlike shape with a very large and elegant gazebo of wrought iron painted green, to the right or south of the mansion; and to the left or north of it, but set back well inside the property's northeastern corner, another building lifts up with two stories: it appears to have served as a spacious stable for horses and carriages. Painted in the same light beige as that on the main house, it is large enough to serve today as a sizeable family home. Thus the Gable Mansion survives with all its noble accessories intact from another age, thus over a span of a hundred and thirty-three years, or a century and a third.

An Island Is an Independent Realm

(For Joseph Jacobo Cendejas, in gratitude.)

An unknown isle in Twenty Seventeen
Is no anomaly—how many isles
Exist but known to few and far between?
Even without historic sites or piles,
All islands have their charms and ways and wiles,
The realms above all in the halcyon zone:
Where winter bird gives birth, and so beguiles
Her brooding time, from northern lands far flown,
Here lavish verdure hath in everlasting springtime grown.

Where the great waves morph into the billows,
                             the breakers, the surf—
Lullabyed by the sea's susurrus-bass, the ocean's monotone—
Here the bearded palms cluster and crowd on the sod,
                             the sward, the turf.

In the shifting zones of halcyon or of halcyonic,
Is the sea the dominant, and is the land the tonic?

A Futuristic Icon of an Easter Island Head

How logical, they magnified the head,
The outer helmet of intelligence,
Those Polynesian sculptors long since dead!
This garden statue-quo gives evidence
Of some refined Art Deco super-sense,
Both male and female, but beyond all sex,
Or gender, might that rest in negligence
According to some unknown law, some lex,
Some fiat issued by some imperator, prince, or rex.

A good yard high, or so it stands, and on its own small plinth,
The artist carved it curved but tall—to prosper, wax, or wex—
And ornamented with a wealth of purple hyacinth.

A futuristic classic, and already thought as such,
It greets us by inviting us, to come approach, to touch.

Some Little Windows on the World

Do sonnets and brief lyrics still have worth?
And why? They grant a frame by which to view
What still has value, or what leaves but dearth.
Ambivalence makes me regret or rue
Which pathway is it that I must pursue
Inside a space too circumscribed or terse.
My means are slight—I have no other clue—
Some scorn these means: what could be more perverse
Than to entrust one's only fate to prayer or poem or worse?

Might we survive by mantra or by motto or by prayer
Such as provided by some sonnet, by some little verse
The needless harm inflicted by a wanton zillionaire?

These little windows on the world enable us to view,
No less than to perceive, which otherwise we could not do.

Winter Scene

(Somewhere in New England)

The wintry landscape, barren and austere,
The leafless trees, can only flout or mock
The lavish foliage of yesteryear.
Glacial debris, moraine, outcrop of rock,
Too mean to feed more than a little flock
Of birds, a few stray cows, and that is all.
In their own turn the glacial markers mock
This vegetation poor and skeletal,
How different from the verdure super-lush and tropical!

And how far distant in the past did such green flourish here,
When in the Cenocene or in the Cenozoical,
When, how did beings get along, or play it all?—by ear?

What flora and what fauna has our Mother Earth not seen?
Are we the last experiment, here in the Cenocene?

Kaleidoscopic Odyssey

(Uncanonical travel)

The Voyage Begins

He had another session with his therapist,
The last part of the therapy was optional,
But he, Jaime Donaldus Byers, chose to take it,
And she had offered it to him at half the cost,
A nice incentive that would help him past his writer's block,
And even more than what the treatment had so far achieved.
Now she, the therapist, was pleased so far in turn,
When she, one Doctor Rachel Benjamin, proposed
What she termed the Kaleidoscope, or the Kaleidoscopic.

The program did involve a real kaleidoscope,
But one much larger than the ordinary one,
And fashioned to be utilized by both the eyes,
As might obtain with some Victorian synopticon.
"Try it," the doctor said. He picked it up from her,
To see no little bits of colored glass or stone,
That moved or changed around. Instead, he saw what seemed
Like changing landscapes, but all of supernal beauty,
Unsuspected and unknown, but ravishing.

Soon Jaime lost himself in this pristine environment,
Somewhere in Roman or in Greek antiquity.
He wore the simple kilt and tunic of a shepherd,
But appeared unattached to any flock or herd,
As he walked towards a nearby temple to Demeter,
Or Ceres, as the case might well turn out to be.
He went inside the shrine, and found a woman there,

A lovely girl dressed in a simple flowing robe,
Some votary or priestess to that deity.

She had not sworn to chastity: she smiled, and said,
"Welcome, Oseitheus!" They kissed, and then embraced.
"Lais," he countered back, a big smile on his face,
"You still plan to renounce your vows, I hope, I pray,
And that there is no problem, or no issue there?"
"I am not a priestess, but only a votary.
I have discussed it, privately, with the high priestess:
She sees no difficulty in advance for me,
But I must find some other girl as substitute."

"Laodice, my sister, could she replace you?
She wishes that she could become a votary,
With someone speaking up for her. Could that be you?"
"I shall do anything I can to help your sister.
Besides, it can but help our own, our lovers', cause:
Is that not true? Correct me if that is not so!"
Oseitheus? He nodded at his lover-lass,
And said that all was well. "But let us note on how
All this will yet play out upon the general scene."

Lais agreed, but then the complications came,
And never mind their parents needed to approve,
Or that the high priestess had cited ancient rules
And regulations, somewhat more than they had planned.
Laodice had second thoughts. It would resolve at last—
Oseitheus and Lais only needed patience,

The hardest test for ardent lovers, like themselves.
The doctor took away the 'scope from Jaime's eyes,
And said, "Do not become too close to what you see."

Although disturbed, confused, Jaime had to agree,
That they could wait until the next appointed time,
To see what the Kaleidoscope would bring about
At the next date and time of day they met again.
Jaime recounted in detail what he had seen,
But he had no desire to return to the same
Environment. The doctor spoke, "Then let us go
Elsewhere during this next Kaleidoscopic spell."
He looked deep in the instrument, and was amazed.

The Trip Continues

He stood in some embattlemented citadel,
From where he looked out on some Afro jungle-land,
And there he stood adjacent to some high priestess
More beautiful then sun or moon: her name was La.
She called this town and land Opar, her own domain,
A former Atlantean colony long since,
Yes, of old Atlantis, and the Mother of Us All.
Here Jaime had become, it seems, La's chosen lover
At least for some unspecified extent of time.

Even if but a simple priest of lowest rank
Jaime in this new life had become someone special,
La's favored lover, Chrysaor, high above the others,

A youth of startling beauty, of intelligence and charm.
This turn of fate had made him thrilled, if not electrified,
To fill, fulfill, the role of La's especial paramour.
A certain competition reigned among the younger priests,
To see which one might gain this coveted position:
If nothing else, this rivalry kept him alert.

But then the fear of rivalry soon cooled his ardent lust—
Was Chrysaor so much the better or the best?
He made small talk about it with the other youths:
They laughed, and said that he did not have aught to fear—
La picked her lovers as she pleased, and when she let them go,
Always she would reward them in some form or fashion.
Thus reassured, he went on, serving her with added lust.
He thought, "Age must be served. And youth? It must be serviced."
And La did not complain, but thanked him for his added passion.
   —Jaime had awoke, he had returned back to himself

He commented to Rachel, as she smiled, and nodded,
"That is a magical kaleidoscope, and how!"
Whereat he told her of his new, his last adventure,
Again she asked him if he wanted to continue
With this unorthodox procedure. He said yes,
"It is adventure I could not have otherwise,
And so much less expensive than to mount a full,
Elaborate expedition, even if we could sojourn
Through time and space as often shown in science fantasy!"

A FURTHER SHIFT IN TIME AND SPACE

Another shift in time, another shift in space,
The strange kaleidoscopic odyssey went on!
He seemed to stand in some metropolis far in the future
That out-Manhattans the Manhattan here and now:
Tall towers rising everywhere, on every side,
Some stripped and bare, and some alive with ornaments
Of every type and style, like gold and silver everywhere,
Bridges and beacons and balconies at every height:
Bewildering kaleidoscope that overwhelmed the mind.

Jaime appeared to stand upon a lesser tower;
He realized it was his own apartment building.
He came up here to marvel at the spectacle,
Above all else at sunset or at dawn, or noon:
Exciting and extravagant but overwhelming!—
Never mind the helicopters and suchlike craft,
That hovered and landed, or thereupon took off
At every height both here and there, and everywhere,
"If this is the future, then please include me out!"

But fascinated, in spite of himself, he stared
And stared and stared; and even yet at the same time,
Jaime felt profoundly discomposed and repulsed —
Repulsed, repelled, depressed, disgusted, and estranged;
So violent and vehement, his alienation
Resulted that he woke up from his active trance
At once, deeply disturbed, confused, and even angry.

He said to Rachel, "That's good. That's enough. Thank you!
I need no more of this kaleidoscopic therapy."

Then Jaime smiled, and Rachel next smiled back at him.
He regained his balance, and gave her his account,
Adding that he felt fine, and content with his existence,
Above all after witnessing the futuristic nightmare,
"If that is the future, then you can count me out!"
The doctor cautioned, "Keep in mind, it was only a vision."
He countered, "You are right, but otherwise it was real."
More palaver, doctor and patient embraced, and he left,
Adding, "Send me the bill, I shall be prompt to pay!"

Jaime thought that he might explore all on his own,
But never did he find an instrument like Rachel's,
And even when he had one made, it was not quite the same.
Some quintessential magick-miracle did not result,
But otherwise he did enjoy his own kaleidoscope.
Sometimes a similar experience would come about,
Unasked and unexpected, unevoked but not
Any the less miraculous for all of that:
Authentic magick does not come upon demand.

But the best episode came sans kaleidoscope
During a strange dream in the middle of the night
When Jaime seemed to be Prince Atlantarion,
Hence in the last years of the Empire of Atlantis.
He stood within the shadows of the Sacred Wood,
Not far from the main portal of the Acropolis,

Thus at the foot of the great mass of Mount Atlantis.
The prince was talking with a Sacred Forester
About the care specific to these evergreens.

He nodded at the woodsman, and he went inside,
Passing through the postern door upon the left,
Climbing the private spiral staircase ever upwards,
Although he often paused at certain windowed landings.
Ever he mounted up and up, until he reached
The little plaza at the top that fronts upon
The Archroyal Observatory, higher still,
The realm of Pharanos, but seldom visited,
Given the endless climb, the only way to get there.

Now Pharanos had served the Archking longer far
Than anyone, astrologer and/or astronomer,
But on this day he had gone down into the City,
To visit with his friends, or with his family there—
For several days or more. Only a few assistants
Attended to this temple sacred to the stars.
All who worked here had to live here, by very need,
The servants in relays thus bringing up supplies.
The prince and the astronomers ignored each other.

The prince walked over to the lookout-balcony
That faced the south, but had wide views on every side
Except the north, with its own lookout-vantage point.
Stock-still, as ever he had turned to stone, amazed
By all the city far beneath, and all around,

The colonnades, the temples, and the palaces.
Releasing an immense and all inclusive sigh,
Jaime had at last found his very own true home;
He did not choose to wake up from his final dream.

Change Is as Change Insists

When in the storm-tossed stretches of the night—
No stars, and nothing but the wind and rain—
The house will shake, as if with rage or fright;
The hearth fire still emits its tidings, plain
And comforting, of refuge past all bane,
And past all bale, a paradise of quiet.
We turn aside, quite like a weather vane,
To shun what leads to conflict or to riot—
Better to see this thing as true, than to deny it.

To not compete, but to develop quite in calm,
Should I resist this natural bent, should I defy it?
To write or paint or sculpt in peace, a precious balm.

To do this is a great good thing, a gift, a grace,
Better than any enemy that we might need to face.

The Miracle of Palm Trees in the Dusk

The miracle of palm trees in the dusk
That stand beyond the chance of ridicule,
The tall thin ones upcurving like a tusk:
Such as might morph into a majescule,
The date palms more into a minuscule—
Their rounded forms extend a place of rest
For bird or beast or man or molecule—
A place of quiet for the savage breast,
For heart too finical to tell what might be best.

A locus haunted by a stubborn counter-contra-point,
An echo that repeats: that is, that is, id est, id est—
A ghostly whisper that attempts an even finer point.

This endless echo in my head might render me insane—
How might I shut it out, this prick or sting of psychic pain?

The Unicorn Looks at the Lady from Afar

I

Even if I can only dare to view her from afar, an extended zone of safety intervenes between her and myself; and even if I can only discern her but imperfectly, still the Lady represents the greatermost peril to me and my well-being.

Exceedingly sweet and lovely, the Lady, gorgeously attired, exerts a tremendous attraction and influence upon me. This I cannot explain, but I sense it as a most profound and possibly lethal danger.

Death might result as the worst fate possible, that is, namely itself, and as one only a little less dire, captivity, and the loss of my freedom. In the latter case I could no longer wander through the endless forest that is my home, along with the adjoining regions of hills or mountains, of deserts and other waste places, of the ocean and her unfruitful beaches, and her never-ending wonder-strands.

Yet I know that someday I shall make my way to the Lady somehow, despite the threat of death and of captivity. Or the best for which I can hope is this: that at least I, though a captive, or even as a pet, can enjoy her sweet and lovely companionship every now and then, or fairly often, or near constantly.

II

Today, this afternoon, I ventured further than I have aforetime, some halfway distance from the befoliaged margin of the vast woodland to where the Lady sits in her park, at the foot of the staircase leading down from the battlemented terrace outside the great hall of the very large stronghold that is her castle.

The Lady seems to be Beauty herself, thus personified, where she sits at leisure in her grand, becushioned armchair, rather like a throne, surrounded by the maidens of honor and the pages in waiting. These latter are all notable for their youthful comeliness.

None but the best and most beautiful young people appear to attend her, where she sits like a queen or a princess, or even an empress, any of these ranks she might well fulfill, for aught I might guess or imagine.

Even if I had positioned myself behind a leafy bush, through which I could nay-the-less perceive her clearly, the Lady looked up at one point and seemed to look directly at the spot where I stood in covert shade. I took fright, and gently, if not imperceptively, I withdrew back into the forest.

From there I went by degrees, loitering here and there, until I came to an exceptionally clear pool with ingress and egress, a pool of clean water fed by a nearby spring. There I touched the liquid element with the point of my horn, to make it even purer and more lucid.

III

Today turned into the big time, the strategic moment, the fatal hour. I ventured out of the forest, out into the open, into the open space of the park with its dispersed trees and bushes, and made my way toward the grand armchair where sat the Lady more beautiful than ever, if such were possible. I had sensed nothing inimical anywhere. But still I remained on my guard, ready to depart at any moment with all due speed. The boys and girls in attendance on her came forward, and abreast of me. They circled and danced around me in a light-hearted and light-footed measure.

They escorted me right up into the Lady's presence. She smiled a radiant smile and held her hands open to me. I laid my horn upon her lap. She gently caressed my head and neck and nose, oh, with the most ethereal touch. How soft and lightsome proved her stroke!

But what was more, and unexpected, her touch was magical, imparting a radiant sensation of well-being throughout my body, down to my hooves, leaving them tingling, almost ticklish. I gave one or more gentle whinnies, such as only the unicorn can emit, a sound of delight that seems like someone lightly laughing.

I lay down near her feet, and occasionally the Lady would bend down from her seat to stroke and caress me. Once more I felt reassured. I found myself in a high state of delectation merely to lie by her side. Nothing untoward came about. Then she made a gesture that I by instinct understood. By this gesture she told me that I was free to leave, to roam as I pleased, and that all was well.

I rose up and laid my tongue on her hands, as she had them clasped on her knees, and gingerly licked them for a little bit. The Lady in turn kissed me on my forehead near the base of my single horn. I lightly snorted and trotted back into the forest.

And thus went the first of many occasions that came about when I would visit the castle, outside in the park, in order to render homage to the supernally lovely Lady, whatever her rank, goddess, empress, queen, princess, or merely a dame of high degree.

Squirrels at Play

The squirrels, one or two or three or four,
Holding their heads and bushy tails on high,
These rodents race across the woodland floor:
And up and down the trees they seem to fly
As if to launch them onward in the sky;
Or at the base of trees they race around,
While their full arsenal of tricks they ply
Wherever they can play upon the ground,
Chirping and chattering, squeaking and squealing—
                                      what a sound!

Although as common as is rare the duck-billed platypus,
At risk from birds of prey, but not so much from wolf
                                            or hound,
They seem to have a freedom and a joy not known to us.

Although but part of the rank and file of the woodland folk,
The squirrels guard the acorns as well as the sacred oak.

An Experiment in Variation

The Given:

Little drops of water,
Little grains of sand,
Make the mighty ocean,
And the pleasant land.

The Variation:

Little grains of sugar,
Little drops of rum,
Make my heartstrings chorus:
Fee fie fo fum—Yum!

The Uplet and the Cuplet

If relevant to humans, then why not perform the uplet?
    First, doublet, triplet, quadruplet,
    Quintuplet, sextuplet, septuplet,
Octuplet, but before them all, the uplet and the couplet!

Or if perchance I need an uplet, outlet, uplift, then
    I claim as apt the apteryx,
    And much more than the unknown X:
We have no wings, and never shall, not yet wherever, when.

No More of Majesty

No more of majesty shall we descant,
But only little things, or whimsical
And unpretentioness will form our chant.
We shall not sing of things inimical,
Nor ever yet of things horrifical,
For too much ugliness exists today.
So, let us chant the super-musical,
The existential, even of decay,
Which like decease is more than with us every day.

No matter, for the mind, the spirit still ascends,
In pride and piety, but thus in every way,
And so the heart finds its own path to its own ends.

As born-again non-Christian, and residing on Cape Cod,
We seek a minor deity, nor Goddess nor a God.

Snowfall

The first snowfall that we have seen
    In something more than threescore years,
During the later Cenocene,
    A sound so soft one hardly hears,
So it appears.

Like evanescent lace it falls,
    Impalpable, and disappears:
Here woodland birds emit no calls,
    Nor melody that someone hears,
Or overhears.

A fragile beauty that endears
    Lays out its gems from many spheres,
A flurry as of frozen tears
    The wind careens and then careers,
Whenas it veers.

A silence nothing interferes
    Or interrupts, the cold distills,
Where nature lightly domineers
    To work her ceaseless miracles,
That she fulfills.

A scene the weather engineers
    Spreads out her tapestry, as if
Envisioned and made real by seers
    Invoking some hieroglyph,
Or mythoglyph.

Snowbound, icebound, frostbound, spellbound
    A panorama-tapestry,
A scene with none or little sound,
    To hold in mind or history,
A memory.

A Fellow Creature on Our Planet

Let us not underestimate the snail,
Some small, some large, as in the tropic zone,
But they all move with grace, and without fail,
Set at a stately pace, which is their own,
And on their ventral side, up-front and prone—
Their molto lento is beyond compare,
Than any largo or adagio known—
They glide with ceremony and with care,
With majesty, with such a calm, unruffled air

What of those giant snails in the Congo and the Amazon,
Inside that moist, lush greenery?—like spiders in their lair,
Inside their dew-pearled spiderwebs, resplendent in the dawn.

These mollusk gastropods have glided from prehistory,
And shall glide on and on . . . on into dim futurity.

Needments and Oddments

Bureaucracy. Machinery. Technology.
Is civilization possible without them?
Whatever shape they take, or could have in the past,
To grow and to adapt, to prosper and to peak?
But without the decline, destined or prophesied?
How much work, how much struggle, have preceded us!—
In this our little hour that seems eternity,
Our minim, our second, our minute, our moment,
    in all of time and space.

The evidence is mixed and too equivocal:
We cannot speak from such a meagerness of clues,
Perhaps we should await another billion years—

Before we can pronounce a judgment or a doom?—
Before we can advance a clear and calm response.

The Elder Daemon

Once again the younger satyr, or Junior Daemon, had convened with his respected superior, the Elder Daemon, for one of their rather desultory but cozy dialogues. He was very fond of the Junior Daemon, the eternally adolescent faun. Distantly related, uncle or great-uncle, the Elder Daemon acted as a respected senior in age and consanguinity. He often gave his nephew, or great-nephew, sage advice, or indeed kind reassurance as eagerly sought by his junior. The former did this especially when the latter was passing through the joys, fervors, or disappointments of some passionate affair with nymph, fellow satyr, or mere mortal human being, male or female not to mention with members of other but closely related species.

The Elder Daemon in particular would remind his nephew that, if one affair did not work out successfully, then many other potential partners were waiting behind the scenes, or somewhere in the wilderness along the margins or deep in the forest. The possibilities remained infinite and electrifying. However, this reminder appeared at times as rather cold comfort to the young satyr when more than smitten with the charms of one very special partner. (Ahem!)

The uncle and the nephew, elder and junior, made a fascinating study in similarities and contrasts. Whereas the nephew seemed an archetypal or classic satyr with lovely furred coat like a seal, curving horns, pointed ears, lower legs. ending in hooves like the back legs of a goat thus more caprine than equine the uncle appeared rather different. He somewhat resembled a satyr, but much larger with similar furred coat, and the skin itself where visible seemed like leather, tough and aged. He had pointed ears, but lower legs like the hind ones of a horse or a stallion, ending in a horse's hooves thus more equine than caprine. Natheless, the chief difference inhered in the horns on his head: "large recurved horns transversely ridged in front," per one lexicon easy to hand.

As in the case of big-sized quadruped animals, like horse, donkey, mule, or zebra, the genitalia did not manifest, except when urinating or copulating, and otherwise remained inside the lower abdomen, withdrawn within the male quadruped's phallic pouch.

The Elder Daemon well understood, and sympathized with, his nephew's exultations and frustrations, more specifically as correlated with his own earlier, more purely physical or physiological concerns or development, and yes, peculiarly his own, as at least being characteristic of daemons, arch-daemons, or elder daemons, not as erotically active as the younger ones.

The great-uncle smiled at his great-nephew and held forth. "I can certainly understand your exuberance and frustration, as the case might be. I had a different problem in my youth and young adulthood. You might say that it was a question of too much passion and the tool, or tools, with which to prosecute it, the tool serving as the basic or prime consideration. A matter of size!"

Here the Elder Daemon paused, cleared his throat, and looked seriously at his nephew, while continuing to speak with his basso profundo voice, but in a charming and mock-sententious tone.

"In those long-agone days, often I lacked appropriate partners, and like other daemons, or satyrs, resorted to other species than my own. As you well know, the daemons bear a close relationship to the satyrs, and in fact claim an indirect line of evolution from a collateral branch of the species leading to your own. However, both of our family lines have often mated with one another. That is why we can claim legitimately a special family relationship, I as your uncle, or great-uncle, and you, my dear lad, as nephew, or great-nephew." Another pause.

"My problem inhered in the condition of species aptness, or inaptness, more precisely. I could rarely find a Satyress or, perhaps the most conveniently, a Centauress. I did discover several of the latter, who found me more than suitable as diurnal or nocturnal partner.

"Nevertheless, more often than not, I had recourse to the females of other species, or sometimes (not so often) with the males of my own kind, of another species, or indeed with random satyrs, always game or prepared for sport with anyone male or female. Indeed, any port in a storm, or any refuge during an acute need or desire.

"Along with my fellow daemons and other close friends, I often visited female quadrupeds, cow, mare, or what have you, none of which ever complained in any fashion. When I made love with willing females, and even males, of my own kind, I had to take enormous care not to damage my partners inadvertently. The situation with humans in particular or with related hominids in general proved even more acute. Natheless, all my partners told me that making love with me had turned out as an unforgettable experience, even if many hesitated to repeat it."

Here the Elder Daemon paused again and glanced at himself down below his lower abdomen, inviting his nephew with a nod to do the same. Although nothing really showed apart from the half-concealed testicles, as also in the nephew's case, the young satyr interjected with a broad grin, "I think I know that which you mean!"

The uncle with an ironic smile nodded again at his nephew and continued. "Good! I see that you comprehend the great scale of the problem. Even if I sometime found its ideal solution with a rare and wonderful Satyress, I found satisfaction more often and more generally with a female quadruped such as a mare or a cow, or more suitably with a Centauress."

The young satyr bowed to the Elder Daemon, and said, "Thank you profoundly, dear uncle, for the lesson in comparative difficulty. I have no problems like yours. I can deal successfully with mine, and I can manage somewhat better with my own frustrations after your moral, or rather practical, discourse and sage counsel." Uncle and nephew smiled at each other, they embraced, and the young satyr once again wandered off into the all-inclusive and all-enclosing wilderness.

NOTES

by Dlanod Yendis

"Only Fifty Times Removed."
The figure involved is given as both 50 or 60. In this instance the exact statistic, only ten degrees in difference, has less meaning than the phenomenon itself, about half a hundred or slightly more, as it has apparently evolved.

"An Achaemenian Munificence."
The Achaemenian Dynasty of Ancient Persia, or Ancient Iran, lasted from 560 to 330 B.C.E.—that is, 230 years, thus more than two centuries, during which enormous amounts of tribute or treasure accumulated, above all at Persepolis.

"By those who had travailed in fact from far away."
Given that the Persian Empire of the Achaemenians as the first world empire extended some three thousand miles east and west, and some 1000 to 1500 miles north and south, those who came from the ends of the empire to attend the Persepolis durbar had perforce to travel (to travail, or travel, but only as a real and prolonged struggle) over varied and often perilous terrain during much of the journey. The Great King, the Persian emperor, did provide way stations and other places of shelter and food and rest for his own corps of the King's Eyes and the King's Ears, and he may have extended this hospitality to the subject peoples, that is, their emissaries and ambassadors, who perforce had to come to Persepolis over enormous distances. The actual travelling always proved rigorous, often painful, and primitive.

"A Victorian Poem in Redwood."
The Gable Mansion, Woodland, California, 1885 (but as perceived in 2017-18 during the poet-author's residence there from very late April 2017 to very early 2018). This outstanding Victorian (Italianate) edifice built of redwood (as was then common) was constructed for the brothers Amos and Harvey Gable, pioneer ranchers in Yolo County (just west of Sacramento): one of the last mansions of its particular style, size, and proportions built in California. This information is taken almost verbatim from the marker just inside the property fence at the northeast corner of Cross and First Streets, a little south of Main Street. (California Historical Landmark 864.) The

large inscribed plaque was placed and/or dedicated on its good-sized brick support by the California State Department of Parks and Recreation in co-operation with the Gable Family and Robert L. McWhirk on I June 1974.

"Winter Scene."
Cenocene: term or name invented by the author-poet (in both serious and playful mode), meaning in general the recent part of the Holocene Epoch, within the overall Cenozoic or Cenozoical Era, or more specifically the recent, or the most recent.

"Snowfall."
Cenocene: see note for "Winter Scene" for the exact same usage and/or meaning.

Afterthoughts

The Symbolism of the [French] Symbolist Movement [mid-1880s-1890s] . . . is not only a fundamentally pessimistic art-form, but one that strives to demonstrate . . . the fundamental sanity of pessimism.
—Brian Stableford, "Decadence and Symbolism"

All human thought, all science, all religion is the holding of a candle [flame?] to the night of the universe.
—Clark Ashton Smith, "The Black Book"

At best the cosmos is indifferent to humankind.
—D. Sidney-Fryer, "Almost as If"

Postscriptum:
Cape Cod and Canal

The cape: a biceps-flexed, right-angled arm
Projecting out and onward in the ocean—
This almost isle has form and strength and charm:
She dares the sea, the surf, the endless motion.
As if enraged by some malignant potion,
The ocean crashes on her eastern shore,
A grand washbasin always in commotion
Not easily approached by sail and oar—
Apart from fishermen, the mariners beware the shore.

With two big bridges and with one big ditch, look! the canal—
A miracle, cape and canal survive the tidal boar—
Howevermuch familiar, they are not at all banal.

In this way evermore to time and tide long since inured,
What number of millenniums the cape must have endured.

About the Poet

Poet, performing artist, critic, and literary historian, Donald Sidney-Fryer is the last in the great line of California Romantics that reaches from Ambrose Bierce to George Sterling, from Sterling to his protégé Clark Ashton Smith, and from Smith to his disciple Sidney-Fryer.

Carrying on the tradition of "pure poetry" begun in early modern English by Edmund Spenser and revivified by the English and American Romantic poets (Samuel Taylor Coleridge, William Wordsworth, John Keats, Percy Bysshe Shelley, Alfred, Lord Tennyson, and Edgar Allan Poe), long after the mainstream poetic establishment had abandoned it, the California Romantics created two monuments in verse, Sterling with "A Wine of Wizardry" and Smith with *The Hashish-Eater*.

During his long career Sidney-Fryer has given dramatic readings from these poets, and from Edmund Spenser's epic *The Faerie Queene,* across the U.S. and Great Britain. He has written and edited more than two dozen books and booklets. He has edited four books by Smith for Arkham House, and three paperbacks, also by Smith, for Pocket Books, in addition to *A Vision of Doom,* fifty of the best poems by Ambrose Bierce, published by Donald M. Grant, who has also brought out Sidney-Fryer's *Emperor of Dreams: A Clark Ashton Smith Bibliography.*

From 1980 to 1999 Sidney-Fryer assembled *The Case of the Light Fantastic Toe* (2018), his historical monograph on the Romantic ballet. As a poet he crafted *Songs and Sonnets Atlantean* (the first series), the final book to appear from Arkham House under the personal supervision of its founder August Derleth; as well as the *Second Series,* published by Wildside Press; and the *Third Series,* brought out by Phosphor Lantern Press; all now subsumed into an omnibus edition.

Moreover, Sidney-Fryer has accomplished his chief prosodic innovation, the creation of the Spenserian stanza-sonnet, long before the recent and welcome emergence of the group of poets known as the New Formalists, who have restored a much needed and long overdue balance to the ongoing evolution of American poetry and poetics.

Although he resided in California during 1955-2017, the self-styled Last of the Courtly Poets presently lives in East Sandwich, Massachusetts.

www.ingramcontent.com/pod-product-compliance
Lightning Source LLC
Chambersburg PA
CBHW071330190426
43193CB00041B/1054